MULTICULTURAL BIOGRAPHIES COLLECTION

NATIVE AMERICAN
BIOGRAPHIES

GLOBE FEARON
EDUCATIONAL PUBLISHER

PARAMUS, NEW JERSEY

Paramount Publishing

Executive Editor: Virginia Seeley
Senior Editor: Barbara Levadi
Project Editor: Lynn W. Kloss
Production Editor: June E. Bodansky
Editorial Development: Book Production Systems, Inc.
Art Director: Nancy Sharkey
Production Manager: Penny Gibson
Production Coordinator: Nicole Cypher
Cover and Interior Design: B B & K Design, Inc.
Marketing Managers: Elmer Ildefonso, Sandra Hutchison
Photo Research: Jenifer Hixson, Holly Price
Cover Illustration: Jane Sterrett
Electronic Page Production: Siren Design

Poetry excerpt on page 47 reprinted from *Secrets from the Center of the World,* Sun Tracks, Vol. 17, by Joy Harjo and Stephen Strom, by permission of the University of Arizona Press, copyright 1989.

GLOBE FEARON
EDUCATIONAL PUBLISHER
PARAMUS, NEW JERSEY

Paramount Publishing

CONTENTS

DEAR STUDENT

You have probably read many biographies since you have been in school. Because no biography can describe everything about a person, a biographer usually writes with a focus, or a theme of the subject's life, in mind. A collection of biographies also has a focus, so that if you wanted to learn, for example, about sports figures or famous scientists, you could quickly find a book that tells about people in these fields.

The biographies presented in this book introduce you to 21 people whose cultural backgrounds are Native American. The book explores their heritages and how these heritages influenced their lives. It also reveals how these people became successful in their careers.

The book is divided into four units. Each unit features the life stories of several people whose careers are related to subjects you study in school. The map of the United States on page 1 shows you the locations of Native American nations mentioned in the biographies.

In addition, a directory of career resources and a bibliography are located at the back of the book. These resources suggest books, magazines, and agencies that can tell you more about the people and careers discussed.

As you read, think about the different cultural heritages that are part of the description *Native American.* Notice, too, that even though people around the world have different traditions, all cultures have similarities. By recognizing our similarities and respecting our differences, we can come to know and understand one another.

ACKNOWLEDGMENTS

p. 4:(top) courtesy The American Indian Dance Theater; (bottom) courtesy N. Scott Momaday; **p. 5:**(top) © Arthur Murata; (center) Robyn Stoutenburg/courtesy Penguin Books; (bottom) courtesy Joy Harjo; **p. 6:** courtesy The American Indian Dance Theater; **p. 7:** courtesy The American Indian Dance Theater; **p. 16,17:** courtesy N. Scott Momaday; **p. 25,26:** © Arthur Murata; **p. 34:** © Jon Gipe; **p. 35:** Robyn Stoutenburg/courtesy Penguin Books; **p. 43,44:** courtesy Joy Harjo; **p. 60:**(top) © Gary Shoidrent; (bottom) courtesy 10K Gold Productions; **p. 61**(top) photo by Marcia Keegan/ courtesy of Pablita Velarde; (center) Shooting Star; (bottom) Steinbaum Krauss Gallery; **p. 62:** photo by Ken Showell, from the collection of the artist; **p. 63:** © Gary Shoidrent; **p. 71,72:** courtesy 10K Gold Productions; **p. 81:** courtesy of Pablita Velarde; **p. 82:** photo by Marcia Keegan/ courtesy of Pablita Velarde; **p. 90:** Photofest; **p. 91:** Shooting Star; **p. 99,100:** Steinbaum Krauss Gallery; **p. 116:**(top) courtesy Mary Ross; (bottom) © Jerry D. Jacka; **p. 117:**(top) courtesy Laura Weber; (center) courtesy Fred Begay; (bottom) Star Tribune/Minneapolis–St. Paul; **p. 118,119:** courtesy Mary Ross; **p. 126,127:** © Jerry D. Jacka; **p. 135,136:** courtesy Laura Weber; **p. 144,145:** courtesy Fred Begay; **p. 153,154:** Star Tribune/Minneapolis–St.Paul; **p. 170:**(top) © Neil Jacobs; (bottom) courtesy Ben Nighthorse Campbell; **p. 171:**(top right) courtesy Shirley Hill Witt; (top left) courtesy the Tohono O'Odham Reservation; (bottom right) courtesy Laura Waterman Wittstock; (bottom left) Matthew McVey/ New York Times; **p. 172,173:** © Neil Jacobs; **p. 181:** The Denver Post; **p. 182:** courtesy Ben Nighthorse Campbell; **p. 190,191:** courtesy Shirley Hill Witt; **p. 199,200:** courtesy the Tohono O'Odham Reservation; **p. 208,209:** courtesy Laura Waterman Wittstock; **p. 217,218:** Matthew McVey/New York Times.

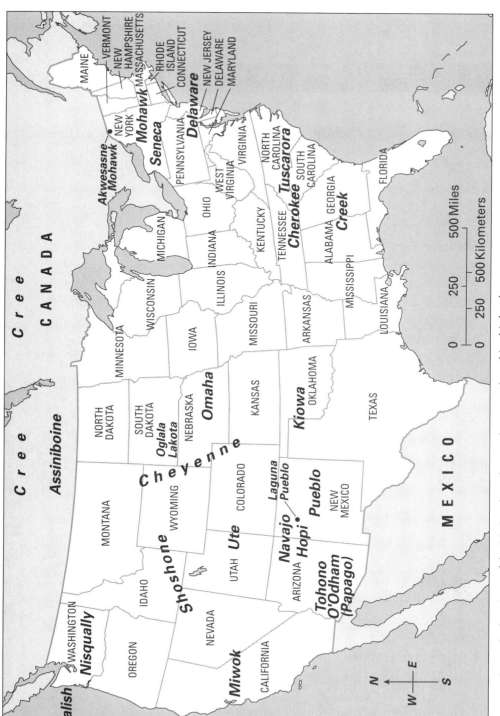

This map shows the locations of the Native American nations mentioned in this book.

1

INTRODUCTION

A biography is a portrait of a person that is presented in words rather than pictures. Details about historical events, personal tragedies and successes, family traits and cultural traditions, and individual talents are often included in a biography to help the reader "get to know" the subject.

This book introduces you to 21 Native Americans. Their biographies focus on three areas of their lives: childhood experiences, cultural heritage, and career goals. Although they are all Native American, each person's life story is unique. As you read, you will notice similarities among them, but you will also find that each has his or her own definition of success and of what it means to be Native American.

Childhood experiences What a person experiences as a child often affects the type of person he or she becomes. Particularly exciting or unhappy times can have a big impact. For example, poet Wendy Rose was teased throughout her childhood because she looked "different" from the other children in her Oakland, California, neighborhood. She began writing to explore her feelings and help herself answer the question, "Who am I?"

You will note that some of the subjects in this book do not discuss much about their childhood experiences. For them, achievements later in life are more important.

Cultural heritage Culture includes language, religion, and family structure. It is expressed through customs, food and clothing, and behavior. Culture is also expressed through art, music, and writing. For some of the Native Americans in this book—for example, writer N. Scott Momaday and art curator Rick Hill, who both grew up on reservations—their lives have been shaped by their heritage.

For others, culture did not become important until adulthood. Writer Joy Harjo and Senator Ben Nighthorse Campbell did not wish to learn about their cultures until they were fully grown. In contrast, artist Kay WalkingStick and environmental engineer Laura Weber simply were not informed about their family history as children. As adults, they sought to gain cultural knowledge.

Career goals A person's goals, struggles, and successes reveal a great deal about him or her. Some of these biographies tell of people's commitments to Native American traditions and causes—commitments that extend into careers. For example, a love for the land is apparent in the works of artist Jaune Quick-to-See Smith and in environmental engineer Laura Weber's formation of her own company, Preserve Mother Earth. Activists for Native American rights include Laura Waterman Wittstock, who fights for equal rights for Native Americans in newspaper and TV reporting, and Billy Frank, who has worked most of his life to preserve fish and Native American fishing rights.

Other people represent important "firsts" in their fields. Engineer Mary Ross was the first woman and the first Native American employed by Lockheed Aircraft. Medical doctor Lois Steele was the first director of Indians into Medicine (INMED). Playwright Hanay Geiogamah founded the first Native American dance troupe.

Still others are remarkable because of the variety of their talents. For example, mechanical engineer Al Qöyawayma is a mechanical engineer, but he is also a talented potter. Ben Nighthorse Campbell has served in both houses of the U.S. Congress, but he is also accomplished at judo and jewelry-making.

Biographies tell a person's life story but they can also help the reader learn more about himself or herself. As you read, think about these questions: What do you admire about these people? With which points of view do you agree or disagree? Which people and careers do you want to learn more about? In short, what do your reactions to these biographies tell you about yourself?

NATIVE AMERICANS IN LITERATURE AND DRAMA

In this unit, you will discover some Native Americans who have achieved success in literature, the fine arts, and the performing arts. What qualities do these people have in common? What makes each one special? As you read the selections, think about some of the things these people have done and said about their work and about their heritage.

The writer and dramatist **Hanay Geiogamah** (ha-NAY GIHG-oh-maw) has both Kiowa and Delaware heritages. He says, "I see the Indian capacity for humor as a blessing. And I see it as one of the fundamental miracles of our lives. It's a miraculous thing that's pulled us through so much."

N. Scott Momaday (MAHM-uh-day), a writer and artist of Kiowa and Cherokee descent, thinks, "Most of us in this society are afflicted with a kind of cultural nearsightedness. We do not see beyond the buildings and billboards."

Poet **Wendy Rose,** of Hopi, Miwok, and European descent, advises, "When you feel alone, just talk to yourself—on paper, with your voice, with your body through dancing, with colors, whatever you like."

Laguna Pueblo writer **Leslie Marmon Silko** feels that stories can help people see things in new ways. She says, "There's a power in words and stories, a power to move and [change] us."

Joy Harjo (HAHR-joh), of Creek heritage, has always felt a special responsibility as a writer: "I feel strongly that I have a responsibility to all the sources that I am: to all past and future ancestors, to my home country, to all places that I touch down on and that are myself."

As you read the unit, think about the cultural heritage of each person and how it shaped that person's life.

HANAY GEIOGAMAH

Hanay Geiogamah, Delaware-Kiowa playwright and director, formed the American Indian Dance Theater in 1987 to help keep Native American traditions alive. Shown here is Morgan Tosee, a featured traditional dancer with the American Indian Dance Theater.

"**A** fiery horse with the speed of light, a cloud of dust, and a hearty 'Hi-Ho Silver!' The Lone Ranger!" During the 1950s, children across the United States turned on their televisions to watch their favorite program, *The Lone Ranger*. Most TV westerns of the decade featured "brave" cowboys fighting "savage" Indians. *The Lone Ranger*, however, was different. This cowboy's "faithful" companion was a Native American named Tonto. Though Tonto was portrayed as honest and good, he usually rode in the shadow of the program's hero. The TV message seemed to be that Native Americans were either the "enemy" or the trusted partner, but not much else.

One of many children who watched *The Lone Ranger* was a boy named Hanay Geiogamah (ha-NAY GIHG-oh-maw). Years later, Geiogamah would write a play in which The Lone Ranger and Tonto appeared. In his play, however, Tonto is in charge. That Geiogamah would write such a play is not surprising. After all, as a child watching those 1950s westerns, Hanay identified with the Native Americans—because he is one.

Hanay Geiogamah was born in Oklahoma in 1948. His heritage is Kiowa on his father's side and Delaware on his mother's. He was raised in a large family that stressed learning. As Geiogamah remembers, "My mother was well organized and oriented toward education. All of us went to school. We valued and cherished it." After high school, Geiogamah went to the University of Oklahoma, and later he became a reporter for a number of newspapers in his home state.

After a few years as a reporter, Geiogamah took a job with the Bureau of Indian Affairs (BIA) in Washington, D.C. The BIA is a government agency that enforces laws and administers[1] various programs affecting Native Americans. The new job made a

---

1. **administers** (ad-MIHN-ihs-tuhrz) *v.* manages or directs

lasting impression on Geiogamah. He traveled to many different Native American reservations and met many people. Geiogamah experienced firsthand the positive and the negative aspects of reservation life—everything from the beauty of grandparents teaching children traditional dances to the misery of people unable to find work or feel self-respect. "I got to know the whole Indian world," recalls Geiogamah.

The reservations that Geiogamah visited were created in the late 1800s by the U.S. government to compensate[2] Native Americans for the land they had lost to settlers. However, life on these reservations was very different from the life Native Americans had known. Their freedom was greatly restricted. The government expected Native Americans to follow many new rules and to make many changes, including learning a new language, customs, and ways to make a living. A number of unanticipated[3] problems arose, among them alcoholism, disease, and unemployment.

Geiogamah saw the problems, but he also saw some solutions. He observed that many Native American communities had kept alive their cultural heritage in religious ceremonies, art, crafts, dance, and music. These communities had a vitality,[4] in spite of hardship, that inspired him. One day, their struggles and achievements would become the themes of his art.

After leaving his job with the BIA, Geiogamah attended Indiana University and received his degree in Theater and Drama. Then, in 1970, he founded the Native American Theater Ensemble in Los Angeles, California. Geiogamah wanted to create a theater in which plays about or written by Native Americans could be produced, and he succeeded. Indeed, one of the company's first productions was written by Hanay Geiogamah himself.

---

2. **compensate** (KAHM-puhn-sayt) *v.* make up for

3. **unanticipated** (un-an-TIHS-uh-payt-ihd) *adj.* unexpected; unforeseen

4. **vitality** (veye-TAL-uh-tee) *n.* energy; liveliness

Geiogamah's decision to write plays was in one sense unusual–there are few Native American playwrights. On the other hand, the basic elements of theater–storytelling, drama, comedy, dance, and music–have always been an important part of Native American life. Generations have told and retold ancient stories. As a Native American, Geiogamah was able to draw upon this tradition of storytelling in his own work.

One of Hanay Geiogamah's first and most popular plays is called *Body Indian*. It is about survival and the ways in which Native Americans help or hurt each other–and themselves. The characters in the play are from a number of different Native American nations. This is Geiogamah's way of representing Native American society as a whole.

Body Indian opened in 1972 at La Mama, a theater in New York City. Geiogamah had opening night "jitters." He asked himself: Would the audience like it? Would people understand it? Would Native Americans be insulted by his dramatizing such social problems as alcoholism and poverty? As the curtain came up and the first lines were spoken, Geiogamah waited nervously in the back of the theater. The audience's response surprised him–people were laughing! Geiogamah remembers thinking, "They're not supposed to be laughing. It's not supposed to be funny." By the end of the play, the laughing had stopped, however. The seriousness of the drama had struck home.

Geiogamah later realized why audiences laughed at the beginning of *Body Indian*. Laughter is a powerful way of dealing with feelings of sadness and hopelessness. It can open people to new ideas and different points of view. Humor, especially "Kiowa comedy," has since become an essential part of Geiogamah's writing. He explains, "An interesting thing happened to me as a just-beginning-to-function-artist-person: I realized the incredible power of humor. Before that I had just been a Kiowa person growing up. From the humor point of view, the Kiowas have a very, very rich sense of humor. . . . You get around a bunch of Kiowas, and they're always laughing, always laughing."

As an artist, Hanay Geiogamah does not like to focus on past mistreatment. His focus is on Native American culture *today*. His primary goal is to get Native Americans to examine their situation—and then to change what is wrong and to preserve what is right. "Of course we've lived through a tragedy," Geiogamah says. "There's no doubt about that, but the capacity to renew oneself, and to heal oneself, and to take care of oneself is always there, always has been there."

Geiogamah's second goal is to explore and to disprove stereotypes[5] about Native Americans, which are, like all stereotypes, very harmful. Stereotypes of Native Americans have ranged from the wise, noble chief who speaks in monosyllables[6] to the lazy "freeloader" who can't keep a job. (See **Did You Know?** on page 12 for more information on stereotypes of Native Americans.) In his play *Foghorn,* for example, Geiogamah pokes fun at the stereotypes about Native Americans from the time of Columbus to the present. For Geiogamah, exposing the funny side of stereotypes can help eliminate them—or at least their harmful effects. He explains, "I see the Indian capacity for humor as a blessing. And I see it as one of the fundamental miracles of our lives. It's a miraculous thing that's pulled us through so much."

Geiogamah continued to direct and write plays until 1987, when he and a partner formed the American Indian Dance Theater. Geiogamah had dreamed for years of founding a dance company. In his mind, a troupe[7] of Native American dancers from many different nations would keep alive the traditions he had witnessed while working for the BIA. The performances would be authentic, and people—all kinds of people—would learn from them.

---

5. **stereotypes** (STEHR-ee-uh-teyeps) *n. pl.* rigid ideas about a person or a group that allow for no individual differences
6. **monosyllables** (MAHN-oh-sihl-uh-buhlz) *n. pl.* words of one syllable
7. **troupe** (TROOP) *n.* a company or group of actors, singers, or dancers

Much as he believed in his vision, even Geiogamah wondered if the venture[8] would succeed. Could he find the money he needed? Would non-Native Americans be interested? Could Native Americans from different parts of the country and with different dance traditions work well together? Geiogamah explains, "There was very little unity between tribes until recently. They were isolated and kept to themselves. They didn't engage in intertribal projects." The only thing Geiogamah was sure about was that there was a large pool of talent–if he could only get it organized.

As it turns out, there is a large, appreciative audience for Native American dance in the United States. In fact, the American Indian Dance Theater has gained an international reputation. The troupe has toured North Africa, the Middle East, and Europe. In Paris, France, for instance, the excited welcome was particularly surprising. Geiogamah recalls, "In Paris, we were 'discovered.' The French people thought that Indians were extinct,[9] and here we were again, like space aliens."

The American Indian Dance Theater, as Hanay Geiogamah hoped, is changing the way people look at Native Americans and at dance itself. As he says, "We perform with an attitude of responsibility, to educate people. . . . We must be sure to keep the integrity and reality of the dances and music intact. Many people don't know what to expect; there is a lot of misunderstanding and misinformation about Indian dance. When they see us perform, that changes immediately." He goes on to say, "The dances reflect the living culture, and a vital reality. Indian culture never died or came close to dying, but we have to deal with that notion people have. Indian culture has always been there, and we're presenting it as it is."

Hanay Geiogamah continues to head the American Indian Dance Theater. He also teaches drama at the University of

8. **venture** (VEHN-chuhr) *n.* a risky or dangerous undertaking
9. **extinct** (ehk-STIHNGT) *adj.* no longer alive

California at Los Angeles. In both roles, he carries on the fight to expose stereotypes—even when they're positive. In recent years, Native American culture has been treated favorably in movies, books, and TV programs. When asked about the current "popularity" of Native Americans, Geiogamah responded, "Our society is very trend-oriented. . . . We're always working against stereotypes as Indians, in our way, not the way of the Hollywood movie, not in the way of the network TV attitude. We are making a hands-on effort at eradication[10] of stereotypes and showing the work of our culture. What we do is going to continue, even if the cycle of Hollywood interest ends." The person who once watched the Lone Ranger ride first into the sunset can now tell the story his way.

> ***Did You Know?*** *Many Native Americans join Geiogamah in the "hands-on effort" to show the work of their culture through the performing arts. The Native American Public Broadcasting Consortium (NAPBC) was founded in the early 1980s in Lincoln, Nebraska, to support the work of Native American filmmakers. The group now has more than 250 original works in its catalog. Another group, the American Indian Registry for the Performing Arts, supports Native American actors, directors, and producers in Hollywood. Their work has helped remove some of the stereotypes that typically appear in movies. Groups such as these continue not only to clear up some misconceptions about Native Americans, but to show that their cultures are still very much alive.*

---

10. **eradication** (ee-rad-ih-KAY-shuhn) *n.* doing away with, destroying

AFTER YOU READ

EXPLORING YOUR RESPONSES

1. At the BIA, Hanay Geiogamah saw both the weaknesses and strengths of Native American communities. What strengths and weaknesses do you see in your community?

2. Geiogamah discovered that humor could help people deal with or change difficult situations. How has humor helped you or someone you know get through a troubling time?

3. Geiogamah had to take risks in order to make the American Indian Dance Theater a reality. What risks might you have to take to achieve your dream?

4. Geigomah is using dance to educate people about Native Americans. If you had something you wanted to teach people, how would you do it?

5. Through his work, Geiogamah wants to show that Native American culture has not died out. What would you like other people to know about your heritage?

UNDERSTANDING WORDS IN CONTEXT

Read the following sentences from the biography. Think about what each underlined word means. In your notebook, write what the word means as it is used in the sentence.

1. The reservations that Geiogamah visited were created in the late 1800s by the U.S. government to compensate Native Americans for the land they had lost to European settlers.

2. These communities had a vitality, in spite of hardship, that inspired him.

3. Geiogamah's second goal is to explore and to disprove stereotypes about Native Americans, which are, like all stereotypes, very harmful. Stereotypes of Native Americans have ranged from the wise, noble chief . . . to the lazy "freeloader."

4. Geiogamah had dreamed for years of founding a dance company. . . . Much as he believed in his vision, even Geiogamah wondered if the venture would succeed.

5. "We are making a hands-on effort at eradication of stereotypes and showing the work of our culture."

RECALLING DETAILS

1. How did Geiogamah feel about The Lone Ranger?
2. What did Geiogamah learn while at the Bureau of Indian Affairs?
3. How did the audience react to *Body Indian?*
4. Why did Geiogamah form a Native American dance troupe?
5. Name two goals that Geiogamah hopes his plays and other creations will accomplish.

UNDERSTANDING INFERENCES

In your notebook, write two or three sentences from the biography that support each of the following inferences.

1. There are many different Native American cultures.
2. Geiogamah is not afraid to face problems or to take risks.
3. It is unusual but not surprising that a Native American would become a playwright .
4. Humor is an important element in Kiowa culture.
5. Geiogamah saw both difficulties and hope on Native American reservations.

INTERPRETING WHAT YOU HAVE READ

1. Geiogamah's family "valued and cherished" education. In what ways is this value expressed in his work?
2. How did Geiogamah's job with the BIA affect his careers?
3. Why does Geiogamah oppose both the "positive" and "negative" stereotypes of Native Americans?

4. How did the audience's reaction to *Body Indian* influence Geiogamah's writing?

5. Why might authentic dances be a good way for Geiogamah to teach others about Native American culture?

ANALYZING QUOTATIONS

Read the following quotation from the biography and answer the questions below.

> *"We're always working against stereotypes as Indians, in our way, not the way of the Hollywood movie, not in the way of the network TV attitude. We are making a hands-on effort at eradication of stereotypes and showing the work of our culture."*

1. How is the dance theater's approach to correcting stereotypes different from the approach of movies and TV?

2. Why do you think Geiogamah feels strongly about doing away with stereotypes about Native Americans?

3. Why do you think people stereotype others?

THINKING CRITICALLY

1. How do you think the reservation system affects Native American culture?

2. In his work, Geiogamah portrays the sorrows and joys of Native American life. Why do you think he focuses on both?

3. *Body Indian* is about survival. Why do you think Native Americans are concerned about survival?

4. Geiogamah says that there was very little unity among Native Americans until recently. What does this tell you about how Native Americans' lives have changed?

5. Geiogamah says he was influenced by the TV programs he watched as a child. How were you influenced by TV?

Scott Momaday, Kiowa writer, colors his etching *1849*. As a child, Momaday learned the stories of many Native American nations. Through his poems and novels, Momaday preserves the Native American tradition of storytelling.

When N. Scott Momaday (MAHM-uh-day) got the phone call one day in 1969, he thought, "This must be a joke!" Momaday had just won the prestigious[1] Pulitzer Prize for his novel *House Made of Dawn,* the caller said. Momaday felt very honored, but he was also astounded.[2]

Momaday's award stunned the literary world, too. Not many well-known writers knew—or understood—Momaday's work. Readers familiar with Native American life, however, applauded the award. Finally, Native Americans' struggle to live in two cultures had been given a voice. Momaday could write so effectively about this struggle because he himself had experienced it.

Born in 1934 in Lawton, Oklahoma, Navarre (nuh-VAHR) Scott Momaday lived a nomadic[3] life as a child. His mother was a Cherokee writer, and his father was a Kiowa (KEYE-uh-wuh) artist and teacher. Both worked for the Bureau of Indian Affairs (BIA), the U.S. government agency that oversees Native American programs. Their work required that they travel to reservations around the country. Scott changed schools several times, growing accustomed to making new friends and to adapting to new environments.

As he traveled from reservation to reservation, Momaday listened and observed. He learned the customs and the stories of many different Native American nations. He also developed a deep appreciation for the land, especially the majestic panorama[4] of the Southwest. "My roots are there [in the Southwest],"

1. **prestigious** (prehs-TIHJ-uhs) *adj.* having the power to impress or influence

2. **astounded** 9uh-STOWND-ihd) *adj.* very surprised; astonished

3. **nomadic** (noh-MAD-ihk) *adj.* wandering; moving from place to place

4. **panorama** (pan-uh-RAM-uh) *n.* an unlimited view in all directions

Momaday says. "I have a mighty longing for that landscape, and I can't stay away very long."

Momaday's early years were not all adventure and wonder, though. Reservation life can be very harsh and inhibiting.[5] In the 1800s, the U.S. government created reservations, in part, to isolate Native Americans from the rest of society. People who had once ruled themselves were now expected to abandon their language, customs, and ways of making a living. Momaday saw poverty, unemployment, alcoholism, and disease on these reservations, and this made a lasting impression on the growing boy.

For his senior year of high school, Momaday attended the Virginia Military Academy. It was the first school he attended in which most of the students were not Native American. Momaday adjusted, though. He was quite used to making his way in a new place, which sometimes meant asserting himself. As he recalls, "I learned to exist in both worlds fairly early. Even though, at times, I was the only Indian in school, I was proud of my identity. And I got into a lot of fights with kids because of it."

One reason Momaday "got into a lot of fights" was prejudice. Prejudice can pose a dilemma[6] for Native Americans: to be accepted in mainstream[7] culture often means giving up one's own cultural heritage. Momaday would explore this clash of cultures and the Native American search for identity years later in *House Made of Dawn*. This novel is the story of Abel, a Native American soldier, who returns to his reservation after serving in World War II. He discovers, though, that he doesn't belong—either to the world of his ancestors or to the world off the reservation.

After graduating from the Virginia Military Academy, Momaday returned to his family in New Mexico. There he attended the University of New Mexico, earning his bachelor's degree in 1958. Soon after, Momaday accepted a teaching job on

---

5. **inhibiting** (ihn-HIHB-iht-ihng) *adj.* restrictive; limiting

6. **dilemma** (dih-LEHM-uh) *n.* a difficult choice

7. **mainstream** (MAYN-street) *adj.* dominant or most common

the Jicarilla (hih-kah-REE-ah) Apache reservation in New Mexico, where he met an elderly Spanish priest who loved poetry and inspired the young man to begin writing. In poetry, Momaday found a way to say what he felt. To this day, he believes that poetry is the highest form of writing and considers himself a poet rather than a novelist.

As Momaday began to write, he explored his memories, feelings, and ideas. His first poems were about the differences in the ways Native Americans and non-Native Americans see nature. Momaday believes that nature is vitally important to Native Americans, in part because nature is not separate, something "out there." People are part of nature, and it is part of people. He explains, "The Indian beholds what is there; nothing of a scene is lost upon him. . . . In contrast, most of us in this society are afflicted with a kind of cultural nearsightedness. We do not see beyond the buildings and billboards, the monuments of our civilization, and consequently we fail to see into the nature and meaning of our own humanity."

Though gaining recognition as a poet, Momaday wanted to continue his education. At Stanford University, Momaday earned a master's degree in 1960 and a doctorate in 1963. He then became a professor of literature, teaching in the University of California system. A college campus is a long way from the reservations Momaday knew as a child. But rather than think of his world as one that was dividing, he thought of it as expanding.

As a professor, Momaday shared his heritage with his students. While at the University of California at Berkeley, for example, Momaday set up a Native American literature program. Momaday's goals were to introduce all students to Native American literature and support talented young Native American writers.

The program had another purpose—one Momaday continues to care deeply about—to preserve Native American folktales and legends. Momaday worries that, with each generation, Native Americans are becoming further removed from their traditions, customs, and history. The loss of these cultural roots, he believes, affects all of us: "Our children are being bombarded with television commercials, radio, and the slang propagated[8] by junk mail. As a result, the . . . language has been dulled. Yet, because of its isolation, because it is not written, the Indian language is not so vulnerable.[9] It has retained a sense of poetry . . . that could be a boon to the young.

"My people, the Kiowa, for example, tell remarkable stories full of beautiful and intricate[10] plots with great concern for human attitudes and their relation to nature."

It was while teaching at the University of California at Santa Barbara that Momaday won the Pulitzer Prize. For most writers, such an award comes only after many years of work—if at all. For Momaday, who was only in his 30s, the Pulitzer was just the beginning. But as much as he appreciated the recognition, Momaday felt that not-so-friendly eyes were watching every move he made: "It [winning the prize] also put extra pressure on me. I had a hard time getting on with the next book. What could I have possibly done that would have topped it?" Some critics also hinted that Momaday received the Pulitzer Prize only because he was Native American.

Momaday responded to doubts about his talent in the only way a writer can—by writing a second book. *The Way to Rainy Mountain* is really two stories. The first story is based on the actual migration of the Kiowa in the 1700s from present-day Montana to present-day Oklahoma. Momaday first heard the story of the migration from his Kiowa grandmother. To get more information for his book, he interviewed many older Kiowa and taped their words. In the second story, Momaday tells a personal tale about returning to his homeland. Many readers consider *The Way to Rainy Mountain* his best work. (See **Did You Know?** on page 21 for more information on the Kiowa migration.)

---

   8. propagated (PRAHP-uh-gayt-ihd) *v.* reproduced or spread

   9. vulnerable (VUL-nuhr-uh-buhl) *adj.* open to damage

   10. intricate (IHN-trih-kiht) *adj.* having many different parts

For the next 20 years Momaday continued to write and teach. His work during this period consists mainly of poetry and memoirs.[11] In 1985, Momaday published another novel, *The Ancient Child*. It is the story of a Native American artist who searches for who he is. The search includes dreams and visions of an earlier life. Momaday believes that dreams and visions connect us to the past and to the power of the past.

Today, N. Scott Momaday lives in Arizona with his wife and three daughters. Besides teaching and writing, Momaday travels, often to places he knew as a child. Each summer he tries to return to Oklahoma City to join in the celebration of the Kiowa gourd dance. "When the drums start rolling and the eagle-feather fan is in my hand, it's as if I'm going back 200, 300 years, and my father and grandfather and great-grandfather are dancing next to me. . . . I sense I am where I ought to be, and where I have always been."

> ***Did You Know?*** *Many Native American groups, such as the Kiowa, traveled great distances over long periods of time. These travels are known as migrations. Because the migrations took place over many years, the group's culture would gradually change. As they traveled, they sometimes adapted the practices and traditions of the other Native American groups they met along the way.*
>
> *In the late 1700s, the Kiowa migrated from the northern Great Plains in what is now Montana to the southern Great Plains. They eventually settled in what is now Oklahoma in the early 1800s. The migration story that Momaday heard from his grandmother has been told and retold by generations of Kiowa. This tradition of oral history is a very important part of Native American culture. N. Scott Momaday now carries on the tradition in a written form.*

---

11. memoirs (MEHM-wahrz) *n. pl.* essays that tell about a person's experiences

AFTER YOU READ

EXPLORING YOUR RESPONSES

1. At Virginia Military Academy, Momaday felt "different." How are newcomers treated in your school or neighborhood?

2. Imagine that you, too, were awarded an important prize. How might you feel? What might you do?

3. Momaday learned a lot in his travels with his parents. What kinds of things can you learn by visiting new places?

4. Momaday's great respect for nature influenced his thinking and his writing. In what ways does nature influence your life?

5. Momaday was able to share his heritage by teaching his students about Native American culture and history. In what ways can you share your heritage with others?

UNDERSTANDING WORDS IN CONTEXT

Read the following sentences from the biography. Think about what each underlined word means. In your notebook, write what the word means as it is used in the sentence.

1. Momaday had just won the prestigious Pulitzer Prize for his novel *House Made of Dawn*. . . . Momaday felt very honored. . . ."

2. Born in 1934 in Lawton, Oklahoma, Navarre Scott Momaday lived a nomadic life as a child. . . . [His parents'] work for the BIA required a great deal of traveling.

3. He also developed an appreciation for the land, especially the majestic panorama of the Southwest.

4. Prejudice can pose a dilemma for Native Americans: to be accepted . . . often means giving up one's own cultural heritage.

5. Momaday felt very honored, but he was also astounded. Momaday's award stunned the literary world, too.

RECALLING DETAILS

1. Why did Scott Momaday live on so many different reservations when he was young?

2. Of which part of the United States is Momaday particularly fond? Why?

3. How does Momaday say that Native Americans and non-Native Americans see nature?

4. Does Momaday think of himself mostly as a novelist or as a poet? Why?

5. What did Momaday hope to accomplish by setting up the Native American literature program at Berkeley?

UNDERSTANDING INFERENCES

In your notebook, write two or three sentences from the biography that support each of the following inferences.

1. Storytelling is one way in which Native Americans preserve their culture.

2. Momaday was recognized for his talents as a writer.

3. Momaday thinks that Native Americans are closer to nature than are many other groups in modern society.

4. "The clash of cultures" is a theme Momaday considers important.

5. Momaday feels that a knowledge of Native American culture is important for everyone, not just for Native Americans.

INTERPRETING WHAT YOU HAVE READ

1. Why was Virginia Military Academy a "new world" for Momaday?

2. How might Momaday explain the existence of prejudice?

3. How does Momaday describe Native American language and Kiowa stories?

4. How did Momaday's Native American background influence his career as a college professor?

5. How did winning the Pulitzer Prize affect Momaday both as a person and as a writer?

ANALYZING QUOTATIONS

Read the following quotation from the biography and answer the questions below.

> In describing his response to the Kiowa gourd dance, Momaday says, "When the drums start rolling and the eagle-feather fan is in my hand, it's as if I'm going back 200, 300 years, and my father and grandfather and great-grandfather are dancing next to me. . . . I sense I am where I ought to be, and where I have always been."

1. Why do you think participating in this dance connects Momaday so vividly with his past?

2. Why do you think it is important for Momaday to have a sense of where he "ought to be"?

3. Describe a special object, custom, or celebration that links you to your family's past.

THINKING CRITICALLY

1. Why do you think N. Scott Momaday became a writer?

2. Do you think setting up reservations for Native Americans was a good idea? Why or why not?

3. Momaday says, "I think the Indian really does have a clearer view of the natural world." Do you agree?

4. Do you think Momaday should worry about Native Americans' losing touch with their traditions, customs, and history?

5. Momaday has succeeded without sacrificing his Native American heritage. If you were to live in a culture different from your own, how might you hold onto your past?

WENDY ROSE

Wendy Rose, Hopi Miwok poet, speaks from a podium. Of Native
American and European ancestry, Rose says that her poetry helps her
understand herself and her mixed heritage.

As a child growing up in Oakland, California, Wendy Rose spent long hours playing alone. There were many children in her neighborhood, but they avoided Wendy, and she avoided them. Some made fun of her because she looked somehow "different." They called her cruel names. Other children simply ignored her because their parents had told them to. No one knew *what* Wendy was; they just knew that she wasn't "white."

Wendy Rose is Native American. Even when Wendy grew up and became a teacher, people wondered about her heritage. Rose recalls her students once asking about her ancestry. When she told them she was an "American Indian," they responded, "You don't *look* Indian!" Rose admits that her appearance is ambiguous.[1] She has learned to deal with the teasing and the questions in a special way—she writes poetry.

People choose to become writers for many reasons. Some writers simply love the act of writing. Others are influenced by teachers or favorite books. As a child, Wendy Rose wrote for these reasons, but she had another reason as well. She wrote to express her feelings, thoughts, and hopes. First with songs, then later with poems, writing helped her to answer the question, "Who am I?"

Wendy Rose was born in 1948 into a society that was trying to overcome prejudice, but not always succeeding. In the 1940s and 1950s, many of the country's schools were still segregated.[2] Even though Rose was left out, her neighborhood was fairly tolerant[3] for the time. Still, there were divisions. She remembers:

"I was alone most of the time as a child; I was in a neighborhood where there were many children, but they were all

---

1. **ambiguous** (am-BIHG-yoo-uhs) *adj.* not clear; indefinite
2. **segregated** (SEHG-ruh-gayt-ihd) *adj.* set apart or separated from others
3. **tolerant** (TAHL-uhr-uhnt) *adj.* showing respect for others' beliefs and practices

white and Protestant. Because of the prejudices of their parents (perhaps more than themselves), they were not allowed to play with me and, eventually, they came to tease me so much when we did meet, that I chose, also, not to play with them. This kind of thing happens to many, many children and it's sad; but one way that such children can take advantage of this is to allow it to feed into them and fan the fires of creativity. When you feel alone, just talk to yourself—on paper, with your voice, with your body through dancing, with colors, whatever you like. And never throw away anything you create. Years later they will add to your sense of who you are."

Rose's father is Hopi, and her mother is of mixed Miwok (MEE-wahk) and white ancestry. Wendy feels most connected to her Hopi heritage, though as a child she knew very little about it: "I was raised away from my own people; I am half-white and it was the white half of the family that raised me. Thus, I never learned to speak the Hopi language which is very beautiful to listen to and hear sung. But somehow I always felt more Hopi than white; perhaps that, too, is because of the loneliness created by the people around me." By writing, Wendy Rose finds that she can integrate[4] the two cultural traditions she has inherited.

To understand some of Rose's poetry, it helps to know a little about the Hopi culture. The word *hopi* means "peaceful," and historically the Hopi have been peaceful—except when their culture has been threatened. They are descendants of the prehistoric Anasazi (ah-nuh-SAH-zee) people, who built beautiful villages of adobe[5] and stone in the southwestern United States beginning in about A.D. 1000. When the Spanish came to this region in the 16th century, they called the Native Americans they met "Pueblo" because of their architecture. The Spanish word *pueblo* means "town." Today approximately 10,000 Hopi people still live in villages in northeastern Arizona.

---

4. integrate (IHN-tuh-grayt) *v.* unify; bring together

5. adobe (uh-DOH-bee) *n.* sun-dried brick made from earth and sand

A number of Native American cultures have been lost over the years of European settlement. Hopi culture is one that has survived, but not without struggle. The Hopi endured many hardships: droughts, crop failures, and invasions. Religious ceremonies, which follow the cycle of the seasons, help the Hopi to deal with these problems. These ceremonies serve a number of purposes, such as calling for rain or a good harvest. Many of the ceremonies are kachina (kuh-CHEE-nuh) pageants. According to the Hopi, kachinas are supernatural beings that are responsible for controlling all the forces in the world. In these ceremonies, men use colorful masks and costumes to represent the various kachinas. (See **Did You Know?** on page 30 for more information on kachinas.)

Like most Native American writers, Wendy Rose uses many elements of her culture in her writing. However, she often gives these elements a special twist. For example, her poems have the feel and rhythm of Hopi chants and songs, yet the words are often very direct and sometimes angry. Even the titles of her books reveal her dual identity: *What Happened When the Hopi Hit New York* and *The Halfbreed Chronicles and Other Poems.*

"Halfbreed" is a derogatory[6] term once used to insult people of mixed ancestry. In a collection of poetry entitled *Builder Kachina: A Home-Going Cycle,* Rose once again explores the multicultural aspect of her life: "California moves my pen, but Hotevilla dashes through my blood." Hotevilla is the Hopi village where her father was born and one of the many Hopi villages she visited as an adult. Sometimes, Rose feels halfway in and halfway out of the Hopi world. Through poetry, she has even questioned her acceptance among the Hopi: "Is there / a Kachina for / people like me?"

Understanding one's relation to the past, present, and future is a central theme in many of Rose's poems. As she explains, "I am learning to be proud of my urban mixed heritage just as [other Native American writers] have had to learn to regain pride in

6. **derogatory** (dih-RAHG-uh-taw-ree) *adj.* tending to lessen or belittle

Native heritage. I have come to believe that I represent [Native Americans] as legitimately[7] as any fullblood, as any person fluent in their Native language."

Rose's first book of poems, *Hopi Roadrunner Dancing*, which she also illustrated, was published in 1973. This volume quickly convinced poetry readers that Wendy Rose was a poet for everyone, not just for Native Americans. One reason that the poems communicate so powerfully to different peoples may be their settings–Rose characterizes herself as an "urban Indian." Many Native Americans writing today choose such settings as the desert or the plains for their work. But Rose writes about what she knows–city life.

Many of Wendy Rose's poems are about displacement–the feeling of being somewhere you do not belong. Many people who live in cities feel displaced and find a voice for their uneasiness in her poetry. Readers also respond to her illustrations, which make the words even more meaningful.

An accomplished painter, Rose has a favorite subject: the centaur (SEHN-tawr)–a mythical animal that is half man and half horse. For Wendy, the centaur reflects her own blend of backgrounds. Like this creature, she and her poetry are a mix: "There are elements of Indian-ness, of English-ness, of myth-ology, and of horse-ness."

As Rose was developing as a writer, she was also studying anthropology. Anthropology is the study of how people and cultures have developed. Not many Native Americans have become anthropologists. In fact, a number of Native American leaders are critical of anthropologists. They feel that anthro-pologists treat culture as a thing of the past rather than as a living reality. Once again, two aspects of Rose's life were opposed. Once again, she dealt with the conflict through writing.

In her book *Academic Squaw,* a number of poems are about being a graduate student in anthropology. The word *squaw* is an insulting term that some people once used to describe Native

---

7. **legitimately** (luh-JIHT-uh-muht-lee) *adv.* in a real way

American women. In a sense, Wendy Rose felt like an "academic squaw." She was a gifted, curious student studying the burial sites and artifacts[8] of her ancestors. She felt pulled in two directions, as the title of the book suggests. The title also shows that Wendy has a sense of humor—she can laugh at herself and the ignorance of some people.

In 1980, Rose's collection of poems entitled *Lost Copper* was nominated for the Pulitzer Prize in Poetry. Even becoming well-known has caused Rose to think about her place as a person and as a writer: "The usual practice in bookstores, upon receiving books of poems by American Indians," she says, "is to classify them as 'Native Americana' rather than as poetry; the poets are seen as literate fossils[9] more than living, working artists. I have run into this kind of thing too often."

Wendy Rose wants what everyone wants—to draw freely on all her resources to be the best person and the best artist she can be. She knows that categories such as "woman poet" or "Native American poet" or "urban poet" reduce her effort and achievement. She writes to communicate with people whose ears are open: "You know, I really just want to make people feel good."

> ***Did You Know?*** *Each of the approximately 500 kachina spirits has its own story and significance to the Hopi. The kachina dancers tell the spirits' stories in the ceremonies. Kachina spirits are not only represented by the dancers, but also by dolls. The kachina dolls, which have been made for hundreds of years, have many uses. For example, kachina dancers might give certain dolls to people who have been ill. The dolls have also been used to teach the Hopi about the kachina spirits and their significance to Hopi culture.*

8. **artifacts** (AHRT-uh-fakts) *n. pl.* objects made by humans; often tools, vessels, and weapons

9. **fossils** (FAHS-uhlz) *n. pl.* the preserved remains of something that lived long ago

AFTER YOU READ

EXPLORING YOUR RESPONSES

1. While growing up, Wendy Rose often felt left out because she was "different." Why do you think some people are afraid of others who seem "different" from them?

2. Rose shaped her interests and talents into a career as a writer, teacher, and painter. How might you shape your interests and talents into a career?

3. The titles Rose chooses for her work often have special meaning to her. What title would you give a poem, book, or other artwork about your life? Explain your choice.

4. Wendy often writes about displacement. What do you think makes people feel like they don't belong?

5. The centaur is one of Rose's favorite subjects to paint because it reflects her own blend of backgrounds. What animal, mythical or real, would you choose to reflect your background or that of someone you know? Explain.

UNDERSTANDING WORDS IN CONTEXT

Read the following sentences from the biography. Think about what each underlined word means. In your notebook, write what the word means as it is used in the sentence.

1. Rose admits that her appearance is ambiguous. [Her students said] "You don't *look* Indian!"

2. In the 1940s and 1950s, many of the country's schools were still segregated. Even though Rose was left out, her neighborhood was fairly tolerant for the time. Still, there were divisions.

3. By writing, Wendy Rose finds that she can integrate the two cultural traditions she has inherited.

4. "Halfbreed" is a derogatory term once used to insult people of mixed ancestry.

5. She was a gifted, curious student studying the burial sites and artifacts of her ancestors.

RECALLING DETAILS

1. What was life like for Wendy as she was growing up in Oakland, California?
2. What are kachinas, and how are they important to Wendy Rose?
3. What are two things about Rose's poetry that appeal to many readers?
4. In what ways is Rose's writing similar to that of other other Native Americans, and in what ways is it different?
5. Describe Rose's experiences while she studied anthropology at Berkeley.

UNDERSTANDING INFERENCES

In your notebook, write two or three sentences from the biography that support each of the following inferences.

1. Early in her life, writing became a way for Rose to cope with feeling lonely.
2. Rose's ancestors, the Hopi, have a rich culture.
3. In her writing and painting, Rose uses symbols to express her thoughts and feelings.
4. It is important for Wendy Rose to understand who she really is.
5. Rose has often felt pulled in two directions.

INTERPRETING WHAT YOU HAVE READ

1. How did the unpleasant experiences of Rose's childhood have a positive effect on her career?
2. How do the lines "Is there / a Kachina for / people like me?" reflect Rose's uncertainty about her identity?

3. In what way was Rose's career in anthropology troublesome for her?

4. Why do you think Rose identifies more with her Hopi heritage than with her Miwok and white American heritage?

5. Why do you think Rose feels that categorizing people is harmful to them?

ANALYZING QUOTATIONS

Read the following quotation from the biography and answer the questions below.

> *"I am learning to be proud of my urban mixed heritage just as [other Native American writers] have had to learn to regain pride in Native heritage."*

1. What do you think Rose means by her "urban mixed heritage"?

2. How do you think Rose's life might have been different if she had grown up on a reservation?

3. How can the places people live and their heritages influence the people they are now?

THINKING CRITICALLY

1. Wendy Rose calls herself an "urban Indian." Do you think this is a good description of her? Explain.

2. Why do you think a person's identity has been such an important issue for Rose and for many other people?

3. Why do you think many Native Americans are troubled by the study of anthropology?

4. Why do you think Wendy Rose chose to study anthropology?

5. Rose has said that as a child she "always felt misunderstood and isolated." Have you or has someone you know or read about felt this way? What was done, or might have been done, to clear up the misunderstanding?

LESLIE MARMON SILKO

The traditional stories that Leslie Marmon Silko, Laguna Pueblo writer, heard as a child inspired her to become a writer. Her novel *Almanac of the Dead* records the history of Native Americans in North and South America.

In 1977, a reviewer for the *New York Times* wrote that her first novel, *Ceremony*, established Leslie Marmon Silko (SIHL-koh) "without a doubt as the most accomplished modern American Indian writer." Although these words would certainly help her career, Silko was unhappy with the reviewer's "compliment." She prefers to be known as a novelist—period. Silko points out, "They never say Norman Mailer [a well-known writer] is the best white man writer of his generation. I just want to be known as a novelist."

Although Leslie wants to be known more for her writing than her heritage, Native American culture plays an important part in her work. Like most writers, Silko draws upon her experiences for ideas, characters, and places to explore in her writing. Her ancestry also influences her work. Leslie is part Laguna Pueblo, part Mexican, and part white. "I suppose at the core of my writing is the attempt to identify what it is to be a half-breed or mixed-blooded person, what it is to grow up neither white nor fully traditional Indian," she says. "It is for this reason that I hesitate to say that I am representative of Indian poets or Indian people, or even Laguna people. I am only one human being, one Laguna woman."

Leslie was born in 1948, in Albuquerque, New Mexico. She grew up on the Laguna Pueblo Reservation. She remembers, "I grew up in the house at Laguna where my father was born. The house was built ninety years ago with rock and adobe mortar[1] walls two feet thick. . . . Our house was next to my great-grandmother's house. My mother had to work, so I spent most of my time with my great-grandma, following her

---

1. **mortar** (MAWR-tuhr) *n.* a mixture of plaster, sand, and water that holds bricks or rocks together

around her yard while she watered the hollyhocks and blue morning glories."

It was during these times spent with her grandmother that Leslie heard her first stories and became acquainted with the storytelling tradition of her community. "Storytelling surrounded me as a child. It held together the whole community," she says. "I couldn't have done any of this [her writing career] if it hadn't been for the storytellers." (See **Did You Know?** on page 39 for more information about storytelling traditions among Native Americans.)

Leslie began writing at an early age. She remembers writing her first story in the fifth grade: "I became a writer because I felt that I wasn't that good as a storyteller at the Laguna Pueblo. When I first started out, I tried to re-create the feeling, the ambiance[2] [of storytelling], but with the written word. I remember as a little girl, I felt so secure and safe during storytelling. I was in the fifth grade and I was really unhappy because I had changed from a reservation school to a public school in Albuquerque. I sat in the back of the classroom and I would write and evoke[3] that feeling of being protected and soothed by the story. I still do that working alone in the room."

Leslie's family encouraged her to write. Her father told her, "If you're a writer, you can live anywhere you want. You could even live up here in these hills [around her home]." Other people in her family set examples for her. She was especially influenced by her grandmother and Aunt Susie. Silko recalls seeing her aunt sitting at a table, writing stories. Both women, Silko believes, passed down "an entire culture by word of mouth."

After graduating from high school at 16, Leslie entered the University of New Mexico. Though she married and had a baby while a student in college, Leslie never missed a semester. She graduated with honors. Something else important happened

---

2. **ambiance** (AHM-bee-uhns) *n.* a feeling that goes with a certain person, place, or thing; atmosphere

3. **evoke** (ee-VOHK) *v.* to bring to mind; to recreate in an imaginative way

when she was in college. Her first story was published. It was titled "The Man to Send Rain Clouds."

"The Man to Send Rain Clouds," which is based on Silko's experiences on the reservation, earned her a National Endowment for the Humanities Discovery Grant. For three semesters Silko used the money from the grant to attend law school at the University of New Mexico. She soon realized, however, that she did not want to become a lawyer. She left law school and turned to the activity she had loved most since fifth-grade—writing.

In 1974, her first collection of poems, entitled *Laguna Woman,* was published. Silko's reputation as a writer quickly grew. In the same year, one of the first collections of Native American writing was published. Seven of the stories in the book were written by Silko. In fact, the publishers named the entire collection *The Man to Send Rain Clouds*, after Silko's story. Three years later, in 1977, Silko's first novel, *Ceremony*, was published.

Ceremony is the story of a World War II soldier named Tayo (TEYE-oh) who returns to his reservation in New Mexico after the war. Tayo is haunted by his experiences in the war and can find no peace. Eventually, he turns to traditional Native American healing to find tranquility.[4]

Silko relied on her storytelling background to write *Ceremony.* In a letter Silko wrote to another poet in 1979, she explained that storytelling is one way her community dealt with good or bad news. In the letter Leslie says that the tradition includes, "stories about the other times and other people from the area who have enjoyed or suffered the same luck. . . . By the time people get done telling you about all the others who have lost wagons and whole teams of horses in the quicksand, you aren't feeling nearly so bad about spending an entire Saturday digging your horses out of quicksand."

---

4. **tranquility** (tran-KWIHL-uht-ee) *n.* the state of being free from troubles or worries

Ceremony changed Leslie's life. The book brought her recognition and awards. In 1981 she won the John and Catherine MacArthur Prize for her novels, short stories, and poetry. This award included a yearly payment of money that allowed Silko to write and not have financial worries.

After *Ceremony,* many readers eagerly waited for Leslie's next book. They had to be patient. For ten years Silko worked on one book—*Almanac of the Dead*, which was published in 1991. *Almanac of the Dead* showed that Leslie was not afraid to take chances with her writing or to explore controversial[5] topics. The book is 763 pages long and covers 500 years of history in North and South America. One reviewer called it "one of the most ambitious literary undertakings[6] of the past quarter century."

Leslie wrote *Almanac of the Dead* in an office in Tucson, Arizona. On the door of the office she painted a 40-foot-long snake with a message in Spanish that read: "The people are hungry. The people are cold. The rich have stolen the land. The rich have stolen freedom. The people demand justice. Otherwise, Revolution." In many ways these words reflect what Silko is trying to say in *Almanac of the Dead*. She feels people should know that many Native Americans are angry at the way they have been treated, and continue to be treated, by the people who have taken over their land.

Writing is one way to seek justice. But writing is also the way that Silko learns about the world and about herself. She explains, "Our identity is formed by the stories we hear when we're growing up. Literature helps us locate ourselves in the family, the community and the whole universe. There's a power in words and stories, a power to move and [change] us."

---

5. **controversial** (kahn-truh-VER-shuhl) *adj.* causing a great deal of disagreement

6. **undertakings** (un-duhr-TAY-kihngz) *n. pl.* the actions of a person who attempts to do a project

Did You Know? *Storytelling has a long history among all Native American nations. Each nation told different kinds of stories. Some preferred stories about war, others preferred stories about the relationships between men and women. Some of the stories were meant to be instructive, others were simply meant to entertain. Native American nations, however, did share one storytelling trait: they told their stories only on winter nights. One famous figure in Kiowa stories, Saynday, said, "Always tell my stories in the winter, when the outdoors work is finished/Always tell my stories at night, when the day's work is finished."*

AFTER YOU READ

EXPLORING YOUR RESPONSES

1. Silko wants to be known simply as a novelist. If someone reviewed your work, how would you like to be described?

2. Silko learned about storytelling from her grandmother. Describe a skill or tradition you have learned from an older person.

3. Silko began writing when she was feeling unhappy. What activities help you feel more hopeful?

4. Silko says that storytelling held her community together. What other activities can link people in a community?

5. Leslie's father pointed out that writing is a career she could pursue anywhere. What are some other factors to consider when choosing a career?

UNDERSTANDING WORDS IN CONTEXT

Read the following sentences from the biography. Think about what each underlined word means. In your notebook, write what the word means as it is used in the sentence.

1. "When I first started out [writing], I tried to create the feeling, the ambiance [of storytelling], but with the written word."

2. "I sat in the back of the classroom and I would write and evoke that feeling of being protected and soothed by the story."

3. Tayo . . . can find no peace. Eventually, he turns to traditional Native American healing to find tranquility.

4. Leslie was not afraid to take chances with her writing or to explore controversial topics.

5. One reviewer called [*Almanac of the Dead*] "one of the most ambitious literary undertakings of the past quarter century."

RECALLING DETAILS

1. Why does Silko hesitate to say that she is a representative of Native Americans?
2. What did Silko's great-grandmother teach her?
3. Why did Silko begin writing?
4. Why was Silko unhappy with the reviewer's "compliment"?
5. What did Silko's family think about her writing?

UNDERSTANDING INFERENCES

In your notebook, write two or three sentences from the biography that support each of the following inferences.

1. Writers often draw on childhood experiences when they create characters and stories.
2. Storytelling serves many purposes among the Laguna Pueblo.
3. As a child, Silko had a difficult time adjusting to life off the reservation.
4. Many people recognize that Silko is a talented writer.
5. Writing helps Silko feel like she is carrying on the Laguna Pueblo tradition of storytelling.

INTERPRETING WHAT YOU HAVE READ

1. Why do you think Silko chose not to be a lawyer?
2. Silko's father told her that as a writer she could live anywhere. Why might this be important to her?
3. How did winning awards change Silko's life?
4. Why do you think Silko took so long to write *Almanac of the Dead*?
5. Why is storytelling such an important tradition for Silko?

ANALYZING QUOTATIONS

Read the following quotation from the biography and answer the questions below.

> "Our identity is formed by the stories we hear when we're growing up. Literature helps us locate ourselves in the family, the community and the whole universe. There's a power in words and stories, a power to move and [change] us."

1. What do you think Silko means when she says literature helps us locate ourselves in the family?

2. Do you agree that words and stories can change us? Explain.

3. Think of the stories you heard as a child. How might these stories have helped make you the person you are today?

THINKING CRITICALLY

1. Silko says that in her writing she attempts to identify "what it is to grow up neither white nor fully traditional Indian." Why do you think it is important to her to explore her mixed heritage?

2. How do you think storytelling helped the Laguna Pueblo community deal with both good *and* bad news?

3. Why do you think Silko chose to decorate her Tucson office door in the way that she did?

4. How do you think Silko might feel about the importance of teaching literature to children?

5. Silko says that as a child she felt secure and safe during storytelling. What kinds of activities can make children feel secure and safe?

JOY HARJO

Joy Harjo, Creek poet, is the great-great-granddaughter of
Menawha, a leader of the Creek nation. Through her poetry,
Harjo connects Menawha's world with the present and the future.

Over 160 years ago, in the state of Alabama, Menawha (MEHN-ah-wah) was left for dead. He had been shot seven times in a battle with U.S. soldiers. Menawha, a leader of the Creek Nation, saw a soldier taking the possessions of a dead Creek warrior. Outraged, he picked up his gun and fired. The soldier returned fire, shooting Menawha again. Somehow, Menawha managed to crawl into the nearby woods, where Creek women and children were waiting. They nursed him back to health. Menawha lived to fight again—but in a different way.

The U.S. government was trying to make Menawha's people leave their homeland. Menawha traveled to Washington, D.C., to argue for the right of the Creek to remain on the land that had been theirs for generations. Despite his effort, however, the Creek were forced to leave their homes in Alabama and move to a reservation in Oklahoma. Menawha's courage is not forgotten, though. His spirit is kept alive in the memories and stories of Creeks living today. It also lives in the poems of his great-great-granddaughter—Joy Harjo (HAHR-joh).

Through her poetry, Harjo builds a bridge between Menawha's world and the future. For her, memories are not dusty, gray ideas, but colorful possibilities. About her heritage, she says, "It's not something I consciously choose . . . but it was something that chose me, that lives in me, and I cannot deny it. . . . I also see memory as not associated with past history, past events, but nonlinear,[1] as in future and ongoing history, events, and stories. And it changes."

"I stayed away for a long time from [facing] my own history," Harjo says. "I'm starting to examine the history of my tribe. I've

---

1. **nonlinear** (nahn-LIHN-ee-uhr) *adj.* not understood by reasoning and logic; creative

always known pieces of stories from relatives. But for a long time I stayed away from reading and learning all that I could, because of the weight of that knowing, which means the acknowledgment of destruction."

Sadly, the Creek, like many other Native American groups, have had to survive many attempts to destroy or weaken their culture. The story of their forced move to Oklahoma is a painful example. (See **Did You Know?** on page 48 for more information on the forced removal of Native Americans.)

Many of the Creeks who were forced to move died along the way. When the survivors, including Menawha, finally reached "Indian Territory," they had to start a new life in an environment very different from the one they and their ancestors knew.

Many years later, in 1951, Joy Harjo was born in Tulsa, Oklahoma. Her heritage is Creek on her father's side. But she grew up in a richly diverse neighborhood—Creek, Seminole, Pawnee, and other Native American groups lived side-by-side with non-Native Americans. Perhaps that is why Harjo is so interested in the culture, particularly the literature, of other people. "The larger community of Black, Asian, [and] Chicano people had an influence on my work," she says. "Some of my favorite writers are African."

Joy has also been influenced by what she calls the "spirit" of Oklahoma. "I just finished a poem today. It's about trying to find the way back [to Oklahoma]. But it's a different place, a mythical² place. It's a spiritual landscape that Oklahoma is a part of—I always see Oklahoma as my mother, my motherland. I am connected [in my mind]." Though she no longer lives in Oklahoma, she keeps the land alive in her imagination, just as she keeps Menawha alive, too.

Harjo left Oklahoma when she was 16 years old. She went to Santa Fe, New Mexico, where she attended a Native American boarding school and later the Institute of American Indian Arts.

---

2. **mythical** (MIHTH-ih-kuhl) *adj.* imaginary; not based on facts or scientific study

As a teenager, Joy wanted to be a painter. But after earning her Bachelor of Arts degree at the University of New Mexico, she discovered the power of words. "I found that language, through poetry, was taking on more magical qualities than my painting. I could say more when I wrote. Soon it wasn't a choice. Poetry-speaking 'called' in a sense. And I couldn't say no."

Joy's training as a painter helps her as a poet. In fact, her poems are often compared to paintings. She uses words as a painter uses brushes and paints: to show people how to look at something in a new way. "I love language, sound, how emotions, images, dreams are formed in air and on the page. When I was a little kid in Oklahoma I would get up before everyone else and go outside to a place of dark rich earth next to the foundation of the house. I would dig piles of earth with a stick, smell it, form it. It had sound. Maybe that's when I first learned to write poetry, even though I never really wrote until I was in my early twenties."

Harjo's decision to become a poet was also affected by Leslie Marmon Silko (MAHR-muhn SIHL-koh), her writing teacher at the University of New Mexico, and a highly respected poet and novelist. Silko believed so much in her potential that she gave Joy an electric typewriter. Even more important, Silko gave her support and criticism. One day, Joy would help other writers in the same ways that Silko helped her. (See the biography of Leslie Marmon Silko on pages 34-39.)

Harjo was now on a new path, which led her to a Master of Fine Arts degree from the University of Iowa's Writers' Workshop—probably the top program for aspiring[3] writers in the United States. Many of the students who graduate from this program have become successful writers. Harjo would be no exception to this tradition.

In 1979, Harjo's first book of poems, *What Moon Drove Me to This?,* was published. The characters in these poems deal with day-to-day issues like personal relationships, broken families, and

---

3. aspiring (uh-SPEYER-ihng) *v.* to be ambitious or striving toward

loneliness, but their "reality" is anything but ordinary. The characters are watched over by ancient spirits and haunted by memories. The poems also contain many images of the sun and moon. According to a critic, the moon and sun represent opposite experiences. The sun suggests happiness and fulfillment.[4] The moon suggests loneliness and abandonment.[5] Through the vivid pictures she paints of the sun and the moon and all the other elements in her poems, Joy pulls the reader into the world where Menawha can still be found.

Harjo has gone on to publish several books of poetry, including *She Had Some Horses* (1983) and *In Mad Love and War* (1990). She has also collaborated[6] with a photographer, Stephen Strom, on *Secrets from the Center of the World*. This book combines poetry and photography about an area of the upper Sonoran desert in Arizona that is sacred to the Navajo. In one selection from the book, a close-up picture of rock that was shaped by an ancient sea is accompanied by the following words:

> Invisible fish swim this ghost ocean now described by waves of sand, by water-worn rock. Soon the fish will learn to walk. Then humans will come ashore and paint dreams on the drying stone. Then later, much later, the ocean floor will be punctuated[7] by Chevy trucks, carrying the dreamer's descendants who are going to the store.

Many of Harjo's poems contain landscape descriptions. For her, though, the land is much more than a collection of physical objects. A cloud, a cactus, a rock formation are all "alive with personality,

----

4. **fulfillment** (fool-FIHL-muhnt) *n.* realizing one's dreams or ambitions

5. **abandonment** (uh-BAN-duhn-muhnt) *n.* being completely forsaken or left alone

6. **collaborated** (kuh-LAB-uh-rayt-ihd) *v.* worked together in some artistic or scientific endeavor

7. **punctuated** (PUNGK-choo-ayt-ihd) *v.* interrupted or occasionally disturbed by something

breathing. Alive with names, alive with events." She goes on, "The Western viewpoint has always been one of the land as wilderness, something to be afraid of, and conquered because of the fear." Harjo sees it differently—the landscape is a friend and a teacher.

Harjo is more than a poet. She is also a screenwriter, a teacher, and a community volunteer, often working with young Native American writers. Harjo is committed to helping resolve problems that arise from the great diversity in the United States. Whether as poet, teacher, or citizen, Harjo's message is one of equality for all people. She believes that she has a duty to others—and to the past and the future.

Joy Harjo believes that each writer has a "responsibility" to tell the stories he or she knows and to keep alive the memories of people like her great-great-grandfather, Menawha. Harjo explains, "I feel strongly that I have a responsibility to all the sources that I am: to all past and future ancestors, to my home country, to all places that I touch down on and that are myself, to all voices, all women, all of my tribe, all people, all earth, and beyond that to all beginnings and endings. In a strange kind of sense it frees me to live in myself, to be able to speak, to have voice, because I have to; it is my survival."

> ***Did You Know?*** *Between 1828 and 1842, thousands of Native Americans were forced to leave their homelands in the eastern United States and move to Indian Territory. The Creeks were among the first to lose their homes and lands and be forced to move west. While many Creeks lost their lives along the way, their trip was not as tragic as the forced removal of the Cherokee in the winter of 1838. The U.S. soldiers who accompanied the Cherokee on this 800-mile trek did not provide them with enough food, shelter, and medicine. As a result, thousands of Cherokee men, women, and children died from disease or starvation. Their famous journey is now known as the "Trail of Tears."*

AFTER YOU READ

EXPLORING YOUR RESPONSES

1. Joy Harjo feels a responsibility towards "all past and future ancestors." What responsibilities do you think people have toward people who will be living in future generations?

2. Harjo uses words "as a painter uses brushes and paint." Write a paragraph in which you use words to "paint" a picture.

3. Leslie Marmon Silko encouraged Harjo to write. What might you do to encourage someone to achieve a goal?

4. Joy never knew Menawha, but he has had a strong effect on her life and art. Tell about one person you have never met who has had a strong effect on your life.

5. The sun and the moon can be used to represent opposite feelings. Which natural objects would you use to represent the feelings of happiness and of sadness? Explain your choices.

UNDERSTANDING WORDS IN CONTEXT

Read the following sentences from the biography. Think about what each underlined word means. In your notebook, write what the word means as it is used in the sentence.

1. "I just finished a poem today. It's about trying to find the way back [to Oklahoma]. But it's a different place, a mythical place. It's a spiritual landscape that Oklahoma is a part of–I always see Oklahoma as my mother, my motherland."

2. The University of Iowa's Writer's Workshop [is] probably the top program for aspiring writers in the United States. Many of the students who graduate from this program have become successful writers.

3. According to a critic, the moon and sun represent opposite experiences. The sun suggests happiness and fulfillment. The moon suggests loneliness and abandonment.

4. She has also collaborated with a photographer, Stephen Strom, on *Secrets from the Center of the World*.

5. "I also see memory as not associated with past history, past events, but nonlinear, as in future and ongoing history, events, and stories. And it changes."

RECALLING DETAILS

1. Why did Menawha go to Washington, D.C.?

2. What happened to Native Americans as a result of their forced removal to Indian Territory?

3. Why did Harjo decide to focus on writing instead of painting?

4. Describe Joy's feelings for Oklahoma.

5. How did Leslie Marmon Silko affect Harjo's life?

UNDERSTANDING INFERENCES

In your notebook, write two or three sentences from the biography that support each of the following inferences.

1. Education is important to Joy Harjo.

2. Harjo weaves the past, present, and future into her poems.

3. Helping people is important to Harjo.

4. Through her poetry, Harjo expresses her concern for and appreciation of nature.

5. Harjo has been influenced by cultures different from her own.

INTERPRETING WHAT YOU HAVE READ

1. What does the "removal policy" tell you about the ways the U.S. government viewed Native Americans?

2. Harjo believes she has been influenced by the "spirit" of Oklahoma. What do you think the "spirit" of Oklahoma is?

3. How does Harjo's poetry reflect her ancestry?

4. Besides their ancestry, what do Harjo and Menawha share?

5. Joy says that from the "Western viewpoint" the land is something to be afraid of and conquered. How does this viewpoint contrast with her own?

ANALYZING QUOTATIONS

Read the following quotation from the biography and answer the questions below.

> "I feel strongly that I have a responsibility to all the sources that I am: to all past and future ancestors, to my home country, to all places that I touch down on and that are myself, to all voices, all women, all of my tribe, all people, all earth, and beyond that to all beginnings and endings."

1. Why might Harjo "have a responsibility" to all these things?

2. What kind of responsibility could a person have to "beginnings and endings"?

3. In what ways might you help people living in the future?

THINKING CRITICALLY

1. In what sense does Harjo's work bridge the gap between the future and the past?

2. Why do you think Menawha went to Washington after the terrible experience he lived through?

3. People from many cultures lived in Joy's neighborhood. In what ways might this influence a writer's work?

4. As a young woman, Harjo discovered "the power of words." What kind of power does poetry have?

5. Harjo believes she must keep the memory of her great-great-grandfather Menawha alive. How might you keep alive the memory of someone who meant a lot to you?

CULTURAL CONNECTIONS

Thinking About What People Do

1. Many people can remember turning points in their lives. Choose one of the writers from this unit and draw a timeline of his or her life, highlighting what you consider to be its turning points.

2. Each of the writers in this unit has felt "left out" of U.S. society. Imagine that one of them did not feel this way and write a paragraph describing how his or her life might be different.

3. Imagine that you are one of the people in this unit. You have been invited to another country to speak to the people about your experiences as a Native American. Give a short speech about your successes and your frustrations.

Thinking About Culture

1. There are many Native American nations. Discuss the common threads you see among the five groups represented in this unit.

2. What are some of the differences and similarities between growing up as a Native American on a reservation and in a mixed society? Give examples from the biographies.

3. Each of the writers in this unit feels strong ties to his or her heritage. Choose one writer and explain how that person's heritage has been important to his or her life.

4. What barriers or obstacles did these writers face because of their background? Are some of these barriers common to other groups? Give reasons for your answers.

Building Research Skills

Work with a partner to complete the following activity.

Choose one of the writers in the unit whose work seems especially interesting to you. Make a list of questions you would like answered. Your questions might include:

⭐ What kind of literature does the person write—poetry, nonfiction, fiction, or drama?

> **Hint:** The Bibliography at the back of this book will give you ideas about articles and books to help you begin your research.

⭐ How do the writers personal experiences influence his or her work?

⭐ What can you learn about the writer's culture from his or her work?

⭐ What style or styles does the writer use?

> **Hint:** At the library, use the card catalog or computer data base to find books or articles by the writer and by other people who have written about his or her work.

⭐ What themes does the writer explore?

Next, go to the library to research your writer.

If you can find several of the person's writings, read the first few pages of each or read a few poems from a collection before you choose one work. Then read the work you have chosen. As you read, see how many answers you can find to the questions on your list.

> **Hint:** As you read, jot down a few notes to help you remember details that interest you.

Next, write a short report. If possible, include a passage from your writer's work. Share your report with the class.

Extending Your Studies

SOCIAL STUDIES **Your task:** *To create a class chart that explains how the natural resources of an area affect its artifacts.* Artifacts, as you learned in reading the biography of Wendy Rose, are objects made by humans. These objects often include tools, containers, and weapons. Before there were stores, people had to use the resources they found on the land to make these useful items. If their land contained a great deal of clay, they made clay pottery. If their land had meadows of tall grass, they wove baskets.

With two other students, go to the library and find pictures of the artifacts of one Native American nation. Write a description of each artifact, asking yourself:

☆ What resources were used to make it?

☆ How was it made?

☆ How was it decorated?

☆ How was it used?

Compare your descriptions of the four artifacts by making a list of their similarities and differences. What can you infer about the land on which the nation lived?

Finally, create a class chart that reveals how the natural resources of Native American nations affected the development of their artifacts.

LANGUAGE ARTS **Your task:** *To write a play.* As you read in this unit, Hanay Geiogamah is a playwright. What are the building blocks, or elements, of a play? Playwrights create *characters* who speak *dialogue*. They describe the *settings* where the play takes place and write *stage directions* that tell the characters what to do and how to say their lines. The play's action is its *plot*.

Work with three or four classmates to write a play. When performed, your play should last 5 minutes or less and should contain a part for each member of your group.

First, decide what you will write about. Brainstorm an idea or try one of the following:

☆ Two friends are involved in an argument. Their friends try to help each one see the other's point of view. Write a play about how the two friends resolve their differences.

☆ Someone is spreading rumors about a student in your school. Write a play about how the rumors started and how the person's friends step in to help.

Now determine the characters, dialogue, setting, plot, and stage directions you will use. Then write your play. Read the play aloud as you write to make sure that the dialogue sounds natural. After your writing is complete, perform your play for the class.

SOCIAL STUDIES **Your task:** *To take an oral history.* To learn about his ancestors, N. Scott Momaday recorded the words of many older Kiowa. This is known as *taking an oral history.*

Work with another student to take an oral history of someone who has lived in your community for at least five years. Brainstorm with your partner to decide what you want to learn, then write a list of questions you will ask. You might use the following questions to get started:

☆ What do you like best about your community?

☆ What changes have you seen in your community?

☆ How did you come to live in this community?

With your subject's permission, tape your oral history. Then write a summary of what you have learned and present it to the class. Play excerpts of your tape to illustrate your points. Discuss how hearing a person's voice can help you to better understand his or her comments.

WRITING WORKSHOP

When a person writes about himself or herself, it is called an **autobiography**. In many ways, writing about yourself may not seem difficult. After all, who knows you better than you know yourself? Yet autobiographical writing can be challenging, too.

In this lesson, you will write an **autobiographical essay** about one event in your life that reveals something about your personality or attitude. In your essay, you will share your thoughts with classmates. Another student will help you edit your work. Having someone else's point of view will help you ensure that your work makes sense and is enjoyable to read.

PREWRITING

Before you begin to write, think about your topic, organize your thoughts, and take notes. This first step in the writing process is called *prewriting*. You can use several different prewriting strategies to get started. Here are two suggestions.

Listing: On a blank sheet of paper, make three columns. Label the columns *People, Places,* and *Events.* Work quickly to fill in these columns, noting any memories that come to mind. For example, you might list a favorite aunt, a quiet place where you go to be alone, or a special gift you gave someone. List your ideas as they come to you without worrying about order or spelling. When your page is filled, you will have many ideas for your essay.

Cluster Maps: Explore your topic further by creating a cluster map. To do this, choose one of the ideas or memories from your list and write it in the middle of a blank sheet of paper. Then think of as many images as you can that relate to that idea. Images should appeal to your sense of sight, smell, hearing, touch, or taste. As you create your cluster map, think about how these images reveal your point of view and thoughts.

Study the example below in which the writer described a gift her grandmother gave to her for her 18th birthday. (A parfleche (PAHR-flehsh) is a Native American rawhide purse.)

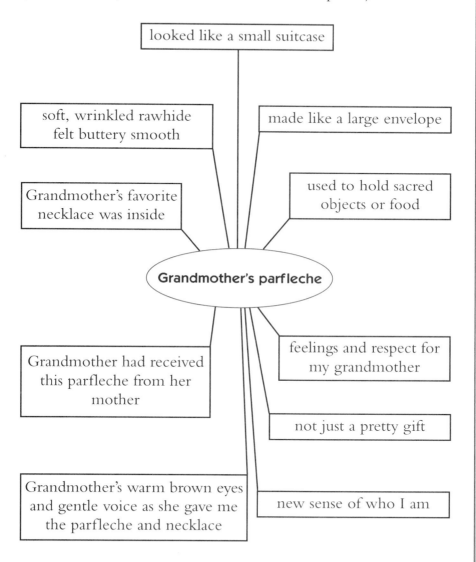

looked like a small suitcase

soft, wrinkled rawhide felt buttery smooth

made like a large envelope

Grandmother's favorite necklace was inside

used to hold sacred objects or food

Grandmother's parfleche

Grandmother had received this parfleche from her mother

feelings and respect for my grandmother

not just a pretty gift

Grandmother's warm brown eyes and gentle voice as she gave me the parfleche and necklace

new sense of who I am

Look at your list and cluster one of your ideas. Jot down any additional details that will help your reader see you and your point of view.

Organize: Next, put your ideas in a clear and understandable order. You will probably write about your event chronologically, that is, in the sequence in which the events happened. Arrange your notes in the order in which you will use them.

DRAFTING

Now you can begin writing or **drafting** your autobiographical essay. You may want to keep the following strategies in mind as you write:

Use colorful language: Include vivid details that will appeal to your reader's senses: sight, hearing, smell, touch, and taste. Try to catch your reader by surprise at the beginning and hold that interest. Be honest about yourself and the things you are writing about.

Use dialogue: Using the actual words of people adds life and variety to your writing. Choose words that help reveal your personality and that of others if you can.

Tell an exciting story: Do not worry about making your draft perfect. You will check for word usage and spelling errors later.

REVISING

Put your essay aside for a day or two. Then, with the help of another student who will act as your editor, evaluate and **revise** your work. See the directions for writers and student editors below.

Directions for Writers: Read your work aloud. Listen to how it flows. Ask yourself these questions:

☆ Is my writing clear?

☆ Are the ideas in order?

☆ Do the sentences make sense?

☆ Did I include interesting details?

☆ Have I drawn a picture of my event so my readers can see it in their minds?

☆ Have I shown my readers why this event was important to me?

Make notes for your next draft or revise your work before you give it to a student editor. Then ask the student editor to read your work. Listen carefully to his or her suggestions. If they seem helpful, use them to improve your writing when you revise your work.

Directions for Student Editors: Read the work carefully and respectfully, remembering that your purpose is to help the writer do his or her best work. Keep in mind that an editor should always make positive, helpful comments that point to specific parts of the essay. After you read the work, use the following questions to help you direct your comments:

☆ What did I like most about the essay?

☆ What would I like to know more about?

☆ Can I see the scene or event in my mind?

☆ Do I understand what the event means to the writer?

PROOFREADING

When you are satisfied that your work says what you want it to say, check it carefully for errors in spelling, punctuation, capitalization, and grammar. Then make a neat, final copy of your autobiographical essay.

PUBLISHING

After you have revised your autobiographical essay, you are ready to publish it. Prepare a title page that includes your name as the author. Then add an illustration or graphic decoration to complete your "picture of yourself." Display your essay in a class Who's Who.

NATIVE AMERICANS IN FINE ARTS AND PERFORMANCE

In this unit, you will read about some Native Americans who made a difference in the areas of fine arts and performance. As you read the unit, think about what makes each of these people unique. Think, too, about some of the qualities that helped them on their way. In what ways did their heritage affect their lives?

The Cherokee painter, **Kay Walking-Stick**, feels, "The destruction of the earth is one of the critical issues that unites Indian artists from varying backgrounds with one another and with their concerned non-Indian colleagues in the art world."

In athletics, **Billy Mills** discovered his identity. Of Lakota descent, he says, "I was never allowed to be part of either culture [Native American or white]. Through the world of sports, I was able to find a third culture and be accepted on equal terms."

Pueblo artist **Pablita Velarde's** murals and artwork help keep the stories and memories of her culture alive and real. As she says, "I remember the stories I heard every winter when I was a girl. . . . They are not legends to me. They are real."

Rodney Grant, an Omaha actor, says, "I'm proud that I'm Native American, but I'm sometimes hurt because other people don't see me as an American citizen as well."

Cree-Salish-Shoshone artist **Jaune Quick-to-See Smith** says, "[My art] is the major thing in my life that gives me great peace. It's been something that I've had to fight for. It is my life."

After reading the biographies, refer again to the quotes above. Decide if they are good summarizing statements about each person or if you would choose a different quotation.

KAY WALKINGSTICK

Traditional Native American values are often reflected in the
artwork of Cherokee painter Kay WalkingStick. The charcoal collage
Early Spring, Boulder, part of which is shown here, presents realistic
and spiritual aspects of nature.

Simon Ridge WalkingStick, a turn-of-the-century Cherokee lawyer in Tahlequah (TAL-uh-kwah), Oklahoma, wanted to do something for the Cherokee people and their descendants. He agreed to act as a Cherokee language translator for the U.S. government. The government wanted to register Native Americans so that their legal right to "Indian Territory" land would be "protected." WalkingStick knew that this "protection" in no way made up for all the land that Native Americans had lost and all the suffering they had endured. But his legal training told him that getting people registered was better than risking the few rights they had left to pass on to their children. In the words of his granddaughter, Kay WalkingStick, "It is our Cherokee custom to consider the welfare of the next seven generations in all the decisions we make." (See *Did You Know?* on page 67 for more information on the Cherokee nation.)

Simon would no doubt have been proud of his granddaughter. An artist and a teacher, WalkingStick keeps the heritage of her grandfather alive by giving people a new way of looking at ancient ideas and images. "Everything you've been and everything you are goes into your work," says WalkingStick.

Born during the Depression, in 1935, Kay knew little about her Cherokee heritage as a child. Before she was born, her father, who was Cherokee, her mother, who was Scots-Irish, and her four siblings[1] lived in Oklahoma. But her father's chronic[2] alcoholism, combined with the hard times of the Depression, forced her mother to move with their children to Syracuse, New York, just before Kay was born. There, with the support of relatives, Kay's mother made a new start.

---

1. **siblings** (SIHB-lihngz) *n. pl.* brothers and sisters
2. **chronic** (KRAHN-ihk) *adj.* occurring over a long period of time

"We were poor, but also very rich in a way," WalkingStick says about her childhood. Her mother supported the five children by doing laundry and similar household jobs for other families. However, sometimes the family had to live on welfare. During this difficult period, the family drew on its heritage for strength. "My mother was very proud that she had Indian children," says Kay, and she instilled[3] in her children a pride in their dual heritage and a feeling of self-worth. Her mother's strength and pride deeply affected WalkingStick as a person and as an artist. "My mother was very intent that I make something of myself," she recalls.

But there were other influences, too. In spite of his drinking problem, Kay's father was a talented man. He was a graduate of Dartmouth College and had been a star on the school's football team. He had also served with honor as a British army captain during World War I. (Native Americans were not given U.S. citizenship until 1924, so they were not allowed to serve in the U.S. Army until after World War I.) Later, he worked as an oil scout, helping oil companies locate oil to drill in Oklahoma. Several of her uncles on both sides of the family were established artists. Her great-grandfather was a photographer—one of the first. "Art was all around us," Kay remembers.

Kay first started drawing as a youngster during the long church services the family attended. "My mother would bring paper and pencils and I would draw. . . . I could see something and draw it. I knew that was a skill that many others didn't have." Classmates at school admired this ability. "Kids would ask me to draw them and then pay me a nickel," she laughs. The future artist was launching her career.

But Kay's teachers were not always so supportive. "I had some good teachers, but I had some [art] teachers who were awful. Some told me that I wasn't doing it right if I tried to do something creatively. I was being trained to draw realistically."

---

3. **instilled** (ihn-STIHLD) *v.* to put in an idea little by little

One teacher in particular was rigid about the "right" way to do things. "If I colored something more creatively, this teacher would say, 'You're supposed to make it blue and yellow, and you put red in there—that's wrong.' Then everyone else would get their picture hung up—except me. But it didn't really matter because I had so much support at home. I saw lots of art at home through my uncles and other relatives. I was really fortunate."

WalkingStick worked for three years after graduating from high school, then won a scholarship to Beaver College in Glenside, Pennsylvania. She earned a Bachelor of Fine Arts degree and went on to teach art and painting. In 1973, WalkingStick decided to get her master's degree in fine arts. With a fellowship from the Danforth Foundation, she attended Pratt Institute in Brooklyn, New York. It was only at this point that WalkingStick began to use her art to question seriously who she was and what she was.

"I did not meet my father until I was ten. Although my mother always reminded us of our Native American heritage, it was just an idea. My family, my siblings talked about being Indian all the time. But, I didn't know what it really meant," WalkingStick explains. "When I was very young, I hated my father. In my childish mind, I felt he had abandoned me. When I grew up a bit, I came to realize that I was my father's child, like it or not. I realized that my father had not abandoned me. He had abandoned life. I saw that I was as much like my father as I was like my mother. Once I came to terms with that, then I could be who I really was. . . . Being Indian began to have meaning."

WalkingStick began to investigate her Cherokee heritage. As she has said, "It was important to recognize what made me different. I knew that I was different, but that was good." As she learned more, her paintings began to change. Instead of pastel[4] colors, she began using darker, earthier tones. The images

---

4. **pastel** (pas-TEHL) *adj.* pale; light in color

became more abstract,[5] less realistic. She experimented with shapes and textures found in nature and in traditional Native American art.

WalkingStick is a "hands-on" painter. She often applies wax and thick layers of paint—with her hands—to build up the texture of her canvases. Then she might dig her fingernails into the surface, or carve out shapes or lines. This technique may sound strange for a painter, but WalkingStick's art is always taking new directions. A few years into her career, she began to use bolder, brighter—even "day-glow"—colors and to make larger paintings than before. Landscape—everything from mountains to tree branches—became her subject matter. "I use landscape because the land so aptly represents humankind. Painting is not only a personal act, but a physical act as well. My method of working is highly physical. . . . I redraw, repaint, repeat, and layer until the painting reaches the level [I want]."

In the 1990s, WalkingStick's art began to emphasize her concern for the earth. Many of the pieces are two-part paintings. On one panel, there might be a realistic landscape. The other panel might be an abstract image. The two panels work together to form a whole. "The paintings I do now try to strike a balance between the physical world and the spiritual world," the artist explains. "I have a great respect for our earth. It is the constant, the core of life."

Duality, the idea that everything has least two sides, comes up again and again in WalkingStick's art. "My paintings are [in two parts] and describe the earth from different views. . . . Both parts are simplified . . . but one is abstract, the other is not." Through representing this dualism, though, she shows not how things are divided but how they fit together. For instance, the earth is "ordinary." We see it everyday, we "live off it." But the earth has a special meaning, too. Native American people may not all speak the same language, but WalkingStick believes they

---

5. abstract (ab-STRAKT) *adj.* representing an idea rather than an actual object

share "the idea, the notion, that this earth is sacred. It's really all we have. . . . We should live a balanced life, balanced with nature and with all other creatures, and balanced in our spiritual life as well."

Much as Kay takes pride in her Cherokee heritage, there are many other influences on her life and art. To be defined as a "Native American artist" is too limiting because some people think that Native American art is all the same. Not true, says WalkingStick. Each artist must be evaluated as an individual—not on the basis of gender, cultural background, or any other "label." WalkingStick has dedicated her life to helping people see the diversity[6] in themselves and in the world around them.

> **Did You Know?** *The Cherokee nation counts among its numbers one of the most famous Native Americans. In 1821, a Cherokee silversmith named Sequoyah (sih-KWOY-yuh) developed a syllabary (SIHL-uh-ber-ee), or set of signs that represent syllables, for the language he and his people spoke. Before Sequoyah, Native Americans did not use letters to write their language. The Cherokee welcomed Sequoyah's syllabary and used it to produce their own newspaper, the* Cherokee Phoenix.

6. **diversity** (duh-VER-suh-tee) *n.* variety

AFTER YOU READ

EXPLORING YOUR RESPONSES

1. Her mother was intent that Kay should make something of herself. What do you think it means for a person to "make something" of himself or herself?

2. "We were poor, but also very rich in a way," Kay says of her family. In what ways can people be poor and rich at the same time?

3. Kay's family moved several times while she was growing up. What are the advantages and disadvantages of moving?

4. One of her teachers said Kay's art was not "right." Do you think a person's art can be "right" or "wrong"? Explain.

5. WalkingStick's art changes as she moves through life. If you were an artist, what would you focus on now?

UNDERSTANDING WORDS IN CONTEXT

Read the following sentences from the biography. Think about what each underlined word means. In your notebook, write what the word means as it is used in the sentence.

1. Before she was born, her father, who was Cherokee, her mother, who was Scots-Irish, and her four siblings lived in Oklahoma.

2. [Kay's mother] instilled in her five children a pride in their dual heritage and a feeling of self-worth.

3. Instead of pastel colors, she began using darker, earthier tones.

4. The images [in WalkingStick's paintings] became more abstract, less realistic.

5. Each artist must be evaluated as an individual. . . . WalkingStick has dedicated her life to helping people see the diversity in themselves and in the world around them.

RECALLING DETAILS

1. Who was Simon Ridge WalkingStick?
2. Describe Kay WalkingStick's early life.
3. When did Kay realize that she had drawing talent?
4. How do WalkingStick's paintings show "duality"?
5. Describe Kay WalkingStick's method of working.

UNDERSTANDING INFERENCES

In your notebook, write two or three sentences from the biography that support each of the following inferences.

1. Kay's mother could cope with difficult times.
2. Kay WalkingStick always had a sense of her own ability.
3. WalkingStick's art changed when she began to accept her Cherokee heritage.
4. Viewing people as individuals is important to WalkingStick.
5. WalkingStick's art shows her respect for the past and for the earth.

ANALYZING QUOTATIONS

Read the following quotation from the biography and answer the questions below.

> *"When I grew up . . . I realized that my father had not abandoned me. He had abandoned life. I saw that I was as much like my father as I was like my mother. Once I came to terms with that, then I could be who I really was. . . . Being Indian began to have meaning."*

1. What do you think Kay means when she says her father "abandoned life"?
2. Why do you think it took Kay so long to accept who she was?
3. How do you think people come to understand and appreciate their cultural background?

THINKING CRITICALLY

1. WalkingStick says that the Cherokee "consider the welfare of the next seven generations in all the decisions we make." How do her personal concerns and decisions reflect this custom?

2. WalkingStick has commented about what makes an art teacher "awful." What do you think she would say makes an art teacher good?

3. Kay's mother gave her children "a feeling of self-worth." How does Kay show that she has self-worth?

4. Kay says, "It was important to recognize what made me different. I knew that I was different, but that was good." Name three things that she regards as "differences" and tell why she might think these differences are good.

5. WalkingStick is very concerned about stereotypes. What is the harm in someone being labeled a "woman" artist or a "Native American" artist—or anything else?

BILLY MILLS

Billy Mills, Oglala Lakota Olympic distance runner, holds a child at the Pine Ridge Reservation in South Dakota. After setting an Olympic record in the 10,000-meter race, Mills was honored by his people.

On a wet October morning in 1964, Billy Mills anxiously walked to the Olympic Track and Field Stadium in Tokyo (TOH-kee-oh), Japan, and positioned himself for the race of his life. In the stadium, 80,000 spectators turned to watch the assembled runners. But only a few of those eyes focused on him. Mills was an unknown racing against what many considered the greatest field of runners ever assembled. Some questioned whether Billy was good enough to compete in the Olympics. A U.S. runner had not won an Olympic medal in the 10,000-meter run since 1912. In that year, Louis Tewanima (too-aw-NEE-muh) won the Silver Medal. Although Mills was a long shot, he had something in common with Tewanima, who was a Hopi from Arizona. Mills was also a Native American. He was an Oglala (ohg-LAH-lah) from the Pine Ridge Reservation in South Dakota. Would history repeat itself that day? (See **Did You Know?** on page 77 for more information on another Native American athlete.)

The tree-covered hills of the Pine Ridge Indian Reservation in South Dakota, where Billy was born in 1938, were a long way from the Olympic Stadium in Tokyo. Life on reservations in the late 1930s and 1940s, and still today, often meant that families were poor. These families had to struggle to make a living. They also had to struggle to keep their cultural beliefs alive. Only a deep sense of tradition and community protected the Oglala from a sometimes hostile white society. Many Native Americans at the time felt a strong pressure to leave behind their traditions and language. Their struggle to "fit in" and yet be true to their Native American beliefs was one that Billy Mills could not escape.

This search for identity was even harder for Billy than for most people. Both his parents were Native Americans, but they also had European roots. His father had some English ancestors, and his mother had many French ancestors. This mixed heritage troubled Billy. Instead of belonging to two worlds, he felt that he belonged to neither. Poverty and early losses also affected Billy's ability to know himself. His father, an amateur[1] boxer, was barely able to support the family. Billy's mother died when he was only 7 years old. Six years later, his father died. Then Billy and his seven brothers and sisters were separated. Billy was sent to a government boarding school. A few years later, when he entered the Haskell Indian School in Kansas, Billy's classmates considered him a "loner." A question seemed to hang over him: Who is Billy Mills?

It was during this time of uncertainty that Mills discovered the world of athletics. On the playing field, people were judged not by their background, but by their ability to throw, catch, or run. It was in this world that Billy began to find out who he really was. He recalls, "I was never allowed to be part of either culture [Native American or white]. Through the world of sports, I was able to find a third culture and be accepted on equal terms."

At first, Billy wanted to box as his father had or to play football. In his eyes, boxing and football were "real" sports, exciting and challenging. Track and field did not interest him. Running, thought Billy, was for "sissies." His first taste of long-distance running, however, quickly changed Billy's mind. He soon realized that running required every bit as much strength, endurance, and strategy as other sports. He felt the thrill that comes with passing all challengers and racing through the wind alone.

Though Billy had natural running ability, it took hard work to turn this ability into track victories. When he entered high school at Haskell, Billy was a slight 104 pounds. But the hours he spent training soon turned his body into a potent[2] running machine. In his sophomore, junior, and senior years, Billy was

---

1. **amateur** (AM-uh-chuhr) *adj.* someone who does something for the pleasure of it, not for the money

2. **potent** (POHT-uhnt) *adj.* effective or powerful in action

the Kansas state two-mile champion. He also won the state's mile title in his junior and senior years.

Billy's victories and talent did not go unnoticed. The young athlete caught the attention of the University of Kansas, and he became a candidate for a full athletic scholarship. One coach, however, doubted Billy's commitment and perseverance.[3] In the past, some Native American student athletes had dropped out of school after only a few months. Could Billy go the distance? Was he worth the risk? Could he resolve his own questions about himself and his Native American heritage in a school that was mostly white? Nevertheless, Billy was offered a full athletic scholarship, and he accepted. It was now up to him to prove that the scholarship was not a mistake.

Adjusting to campus life can be difficult for any student. For shy, withdrawn Billy Mills, the adjustments were particularly troublesome. Prejudice against Native Americans was not uncommon. Even Billy's growing reputation as a runner did not make him immune[4] to it. The remaining barriers between him and white society became painfully clear in an incident involving a campus fraternity.[5] The fraternity wanted track-and-field athletes to become members. Billy was refused membership, however, because the fraternity's rules did not allow "Indians" to join. This and other rejections made him feel even more alone. The temptation to quit school was strong.

Despite these difficulties, though, Billy held on and began to win races for the University of Kansas track team. He was a member of the team that won the National Track Championship two years in a row. Billy himself was a Big Eight cross-country champion. At one meet he set a conference record of 31 minutes for the 10,000-meter run. In 1955, his final year at the university,

---

3. **perseverance** (per-suh-VIHR-uhns) *n.* continued, patient effort

4. **immune** (ih-MYOON) *adj.* protected against something disagreeable or harmful

5. **fraternity** (fruh-TERN-uh-tee) *n.* a group of young men joined by common interests; a Greek-letter college organization

Billy began to lose races. It was during this troubled time that Billy first tried out for the Olympic team. When he did not make the team, he turned his back on running. Reflecting on why he began to lose, Billy remembers, "I didn't realize it then, but it was because of my attitude. I just didn't want to make the effort. I wasn't interested and because I wasn't, it was impossible for me to win. I blocked myself off from winning."

Mills did graduate, however, and soon after he married a college classmate and accepted a commission[6] in the Marine Corps. After a few years, one of Billy's fellow officers in Camp Pendleton, in southern California, convinced him to run again. Billy began to rebuild the endurance that long-distance running requires. It was not long before he was winning again. He won the interservice 10,000-meter run in Germany, and trimmed his mile time to 4 minutes, 6 seconds.

Billy trained even harder. In 1963, one year before the games in Tokyo, he began running twice a day, seven days a week. His total mileage zoomed from 40 to 100 miles a week. The Marine Corps sponsored Billy's trip to the Olympic trials, where his training paid off. He qualified for the Olympic team in the marathon (a long run of a little more than 26 miles) and the 10,000-meter run.

Yet even as a member of the U.S. Olympic team, Billy felt like an outsider. Just minutes before the 10,000-meter race began, the U.S. track coach came into the locker room that Billy shared with fellow American Gerry Lindgren. Gerry was considered the United States' best chance to win. The coach had come to discuss the 10 runners he believed stood between Lindgren and the Gold Medal. Mills's name was not among them. Billy recalls, "I kept hoping he would mention my name in the top 10, but it didn't appear."

As the race began, the crowded field of runners lived up to its reputation as the fastest in Olympic history. Ron Clarke of

---

6. commission (kuh-MIHSH-uhn) *n.* a document issued by the President, making a person an officer in the U.S. armed forces

Australia, the world-record holder for the 10,000-meter run, overtook Lindgren at the 5,000 mark. Clarke's lead was expected. That Billy Mills was in close pursuit, however, was unexpected. The final laps became a three-man race among Clarke, Mohammed Gammoudi (moh-HAHM-ihd ga-MOO-dih) of Tunisia, and Billy Mills. In the first turn of the last lap, Gammoudi bumped Clarke, who then sent Billy careening[7] into the third lane. Mills was now a very long 20 yards behind.

It was then that all of Billy's hopes and beliefs came together. Billy recalls, "I felt this incredible strength within me, and I started to think, 'I can win, I can win, I can win,' over and over in my mind. I had visualized winning the race over in my mind many times as I had trained and saw myself overcome the leaders right at the last." With a sudden explosion of speed, Billy Mills began to move ahead. The announcer of the race lost all composure[8] as he screamed the final exciting seconds into the microphone. The roar of 80,000 cheering spectators seemed to lift Mills past Clarke and Gammoudi, across the finish line, and into Olympic history.

Billy's victory set an Olympic record and was considered the greatest upset in the history of the games. He came home to victory parades and instant fame. He was a hero, and to no one more than his people, the Lakota. On the Pine Ridge Reservation, a traditional powwow[9] was held to honor the young man who had gone away like a warrior to win his eagle feathers. His people gave Billy a ring made of gold mined from the Black Hills, their sacred land. "The ring is one of my most cherished possessions," says Billy, "because it is something I can wear and show people that I am proud to be Sioux.[10] It has

---

7. **careening** (kuh-REEN-uhng) *v.* to be lurching or tilting from side to side

8. **composure** (kuhm-POH-zhuhr) *n.* calmness of mind or manner

9. **powwow** (POW-wow) *n.* a ceremony or conference of Native Americans to help cure disease or celebrate success, often with feasting and dancing

10. **Sioux** (SOO) *n.* refers to the Oglala Lakota nation of Native Americans

much greater meaning for me than the Olympic gold medal, although that is cherished too."

What finally drove Billy Mills to victory? Was it simply a question of physical training? Had he finally overcome his doubts about what he wanted and who he was? Perhaps an incident just minutes after Billy's breathtaking finish contains the answer. His victory was so unexpected that the Japanese Olympic officials did not recognize the winner. Billy remembers, "The Japanese judge kept asking me, 'You are? You are?' For the first time in my life I could look at someone in the eyes and tell them who I really was."

Today Billy Mills own his own insurance company in Sacramento, California. He remembers fondly all the places his life has taken him. Perhaps his favorite place, however, is that track in Tokyo where he "found himself."

Did You Know? *Another Native American "discovered the world of athletics" while attending a government boarding school. Jim Thorpe played football, track, and baseball at the Carlisle Indian School beginning in 1907. His athletic ability is often discussed with awe. In fact, he is considered to be one of the greatest all-around athletes of all time. Thorpe went on to win the decathalon and pentathlon at the Olympics in 1912, the same year Louis Tewanima won the 10,000-meter run.*

AFTER YOU READ

EXPLORING YOUR RESPONSES

1. Billy Mills had natural ability as a runner, but training and practice turned this ability into success. How might training and practice help you achieve your goals?

2. Billy had difficulty adjusting to the University of Kansas, but he was able to win some important races. Describe a time when you or someone you know succeeded in a difficult situation.

3. Billy began to lose races in 1955, as he says, "because of my attitude." Describe a time when attitude made a difference in whether you or someone you know achieved a goal.

4. After winning the Olympics, Billy said, "For the first time in my life I could [say] . . . who I really was." What might you say if someone asked you the same question?

5. Being separated from his family made Billy feel lonely and uncertain. How might you have suggested that he understand or overcome these feelings?

UNDERSTANDING WORDS IN CONTEXT

Read the following sentences from the biography. Think about what each underlined word means. In your notebook, write what the word means as it is used in the sentence.

1. One coach, however, doubted Billy's commitment and perseverance.

2. Prejudice against Native Americans was not uncommon. Even Billy's growing reputation as a runner did not make him immune to it.

3. On the Pine Ridge Reservation, a traditional powwow was held to honor the young man who had gone away like a warrior to win his eagle feathers.

4. In the first turn of the last lap, Gammoudi bumped Clarke, who then sent Billy <u>careening</u> into the third lane.

5. The announcer of the race lost all <u>composure</u> as he screamed the final exciting seconds into the microphone.

RECALLING DETAILS

1. Why was Billy sent to a government boarding school?
2. Why did Billy Mills decide to become a long-distance runner?
3. List at least three significant events in Mills's life after college.
4. Describe the 10,000-meter race in the 1964 Olympics.
5. How did the Oglala react to Billy's success?

UNDERSTANDING INFERENCES

In your notebook, write two or three sentences from the biography that support each of the following inferences.

1. For many years, Billy felt uncertain about who he was and where he belonged.
2. Billy worked hard and had a competitive spirit.
3. Attitude is an important element in achieving a goal.
4. Mills's Olympic experience helped him understand who he was.
5. Billy Mills received support and encouragement from others.

INTERPRETING WHAT YOU HAVE READ

1. Why was the world of sports a good place for Billy to discover who he was?
2. Why do you think some Native American athletes had dropped out of the University of Kansas before Billy attended the school?
3. How did Billy deal with the prejudice he encountered?
4. Why do you think Mills was able to come from behind and win the gold medal in Tokyo?

5. Billy had something in common with silver medalist Lewis Tewanima. Do you think Tewanima might have been a role model for Mills? Explain.

ANALYZING QUOTATIONS

Read the following quotation from the biography and answer the questions below.

> *"The ring is one of my most cherished possessions because it is something I can wear and show people that I am proud to be Sioux. It has much greater meaning for me than the Olympic gold medal, although that is cherished too."*

1. Billy mentions two symbols of achievement—his ring and his medal. Think about their physical appearance. What does each represent to him? Be specific.
2. Why do you think the Oglala are proud of Billy?
3. Would the ring or the medal mean more to you? Explain.

THINKING CRITICALLY

1. Billy had a difficult life, yet he was able to accomplish important goals. What qualities helped him to do so?
2. Billy said that through sports he "was able to find a third culture and be accepted on equal terms." Do you agree that sports can help people feel they fit into a new group? Explain.
3. In what ways did Mills's triumph at the Olympics make him "like a warrior" who had gone away "to win his eagle feathers"?
4. Why do you think Mills had more difficulty living up to his potential in college than he did later in his life?
5. Billy went through a "quest for identity," and found himself in the sport of long-distance running. What talents or interests do you have that might help you discover who you are?

PABLITA VELARDE

Pablita Velarde, Tewa artist, educates people about her heritage
through her artwork. This painting of two Native American dancers
is from Velarde's book *Old Father Story Teller,* which recounts many
of the traditional stories she heard as a child.

Imagine you wake up one morning and you cannot see anything. The sky, the trees, your family—you can only remember what they look like. For the artist Pablita Velarde (pahb-LEE-tah veh-LAHR-deh), this really happened. When she was 3 years old, Pablita suddenly and mysteriously lost her vision. Many people thought that she would never see again. Gradually, however, Pablita's sight was restored.[1] She celebrates her sense of sight daily as she paints her pictures.

Pablita Velarde was born on September 19, 1918, in the village of Santa Clara, New Mexico. Santa Clara is one of many flat-topped Native American villages that lie along the Rio Grande River valley in the northern half of the state. The scenery there is breathtaking, full of multicolored cliffs.

When Pablita was 3 years old, her mother died. Shortly after that, Pablita was struck with the mysterious illness that temporarily blinded her. Her father was a medicine man,[2] and he treated Pablita with the traditional remedies of his Santa Clara ancestors. As Pablita's sight came back, every detail she observed seemed important to her. She remembers family members using the pigments[3] from the nearby earth to paint colorful designs on the house walls and on the pottery they made. Her aunts taught Pablita to make pottery and decorate it herself. Little did her family know then that one day Pablita would turn this "child's play" into works of art that taught the world about her people. (See **Did You Know?** on page 86 for more information on the Tewa pottery.)

---

1. **restored** (rih-STOHRD) *v.* brought back to its former condition
2. **medicine man** a man, usually a Native American, who prevents or treats illness with herbs, songs, dances, and other traditional methods
3. **pigments** (PIHG-muhnts) *n. pl.* materials used to color; paints

After his wife's death, Pablita's father found it difficult to both farm his land and care for his daughters. When the girls reached school age, he sent them to St. Catherine's Indian School in Santa Fe, New Mexico. When she was born, Pablita had been named Tse Tsan (TSEE TSAHN) by her grandmother. This name is Tewa (TAY-wah), the traditional language of the Santa Clara, for "Golden Dawn." However, the nuns at the school changed her Tewa name to Pablita Velarde, a Spanish name.

When she was 13 years old, Pablita graduated from St. Catherine's. She then went to a government school in Santa Fe. That same year, a new art teacher named Dorothy Dunn also arrived at the school. Dunn was a teacher with special qualities. She understood the fears of her Native American students, who had been removed from family and friends. Dunn also had a deep appreciation for Native American culture.

Dorothy Dunn encouraged her students to express their own ideas and feelings through art. She also suggested that students use memories of their family and home to inspire[4] them to create their art. Dunn insisted that her students respect and learn about their own culture. For Pablita, learning from Dorothy Dunn was like having her sight restored a second time.

By her late teens, Velarde knew she wanted to become an artist. A few things held her back, though. One problem was her shyness. It was hard for Pablita to talk with people who might sell or buy her paintings. Another "problem" was out of her control. Pablita was a woman, and women did not get much encouragement as artists at the time. There were great women painters like Georgia O'Keeffe[5] who had come from the East to work in New Mexico. But there were very few Native American women artists.

Fortunately, Pablita became friends with one of these exceptions, Tonita Peña (tohn-EE-tah PEHN-yah). Peña painted

---

4. **inspire** (ihn-SPEYER) *v.* to have an effect on someone or something

5. **Georgia O'Keeffe** (1887-1986) a major U.S. artist who began painting in New Mexico in 1929

pictures with finely detailed scenes of southwestern Native American community life. Velarde saw her familiar surroundings in a new and exciting light. She thought, "If she can do it, so can I!" Pablita was now determined to challenge the traditions that kept women in her community from doing what they wanted.

After she graduated from high school, Velarde taught art in the Santa Clara elementary school. Then, when she was 21 years old, Pablita got her first job as an artist. She was to paint part of a mural[6] that would decorate the wall of a store in Albuquerque, New Mexico. Pablita had learned much from Peña and from watching people live, play, and work in her village. She painted a group of Santa Clara women displaying their famous black clay pots. In Dorothy Dunn's words, "The calico dresses are minutely[7] patterned with almost mechanical[8] exactness, and the pottery forms are shaped firmly and painted precisely, as in life."

It did not take long for Pablita's reputation as an artist to spread. Soon she was asked to paint a mural for the U.S. Park Service at Bandelier (BAN-duh-leer) National Monument in New Mexico. From 1939-41, Velarde researched and painted the history of the Rio Grande Tewa. In vivid colors and with respect for every detail, she showed her ancestors going about their daily business. Farming, building, cooking, weaving, and pottery-making are all represented. The scene is crowded with life, yet each figure stands out from the rest. Here, one face looks sad. There, one is daydreaming. In the distance, one looks amused.

The mural is considered one of Velarde's greatest achievements. The use of detail in the mural—and in all of Velarde's paintings—is often praised. Although the details are pleasing to the eye, they are also educational. They give valuable information about Velarde's culture. Through her art, this information is preserved in a way that makes it fun and easy to remember. For

---

6. **mural** (MYOOR-uhl) *n.* a large scene or design painted directly on a wall

7. **minutely** (meye-NOOT-lee) *adv.* in very small detail

8. **mechanical** (muh-KAN-ih-kuhl) *adj.* as if produced by a machine; very carefully made

example, a lively painting of a dance with drums beating and animals scampering about teaches the viewer about Tewa religious beliefs and ceremonies. The detail in some of Velarde's artwork is so accurate that her paintings become "snapshots" of a time when cameras did not exist.

After completing the Bandelier mural, Pablita decided to return to Santa Clara. There she built–almost by herself–a studio-home. Many people in her village considered it unusual for a woman to live and work alone. But Velarde did not mind what others thought. She now had a place of her own to work on her art.

Velarde has discovered many new ways of creating and applying paint in her studio. One of these methods is called "earth painting." Earth painting requires several steps. First, Pablita collects colored stones. Then she grinds them to a fine powder. She prepares the surface of a large panel with pumice (PUM-uhs). This is a lightweight stone with a rough surface that she uses to smooth the panel. Then Velarde draws her design in pencil and paints in the outlined sections. While the paint is drying, she takes the stone powder and mixes it with glue and water. Then, layer upon layer, she adds the colored stone to the dried paint. Finally, Pablita gives it a finishing coat that contains a secret ingredient. Her earth paintings look the way they sound–textured and colored like the land itself.

Although Pablita Velarde has worked consistently since the 1930s on her art, it took until 1948 for her to become well-known as an artist. In that year, she won her first important award. This award came from the Phil Brook Art Center in Tulsa, Oklahoma. Many other blue ribbons and prizes followed. Soon, her name was being mentioned on television and in newspapers. Then in 1955, the French government gave Velarde an award for her "outstanding contribution to art." At last, Pablita Velarde was recognized in a world that did not have many women or Native American painters.

Pablita's culture and the lessons she learned in childhood continue to be important to her. When Pablita goes through difficult personal times, she often remembers the stories she heard as a child. In 1960, she published some of these stories in a book, *Old Father Story Teller*, which she both wrote and illustrated. The cover is a picture of "Old Father" surrounded by children listening to stories. Inside, Pablita preserved some of the tales of her people. The book was a huge success.

Pablita Velarde, like many Native American writers and artists, believes that the past lives through art. As she reflects, "I sit on my couch and look outside. I have to open lots of little windows in my head—thinking about things that have happened to me, or to someone else that I know. And I remember the stories I heard every winter when I was a girl told by my grandfather or my grandmother, my uncle or my father. They are not legends to me. They are real."

> ***Did You Know?*** *The term Tewa refers to a number of Southwestern Native American groups that speak a similar language. Anthropologists classify the Tewa on another basis: the style of pottery they began making more than 1,000 years ago. Pottery remains tell us about early people. For example, Tewa pottery remains (such as those Pablita and her sister often found when playing among the cliffs around Santa Clara) show what materials were available to the Tewa. These included clay and sand, stones for polishing the pieces, yucca (YUK-uh) plants that were used as paintbrushes, and animal dung that was used to fuel the fires in which the pots were placed. Through the process of firing, the colors of the pottery—red and black—were set and the piece was hardened.*

AFTER YOU READ

EXPLORING YOUR RESPONSES

1. Pablita Velarde's art is rooted in her childhood. How do you think a person's childhood affects him or her as an adult?

2. Velarde was shy, yet her shyness did not keep her from becoming a respected artist. How can shyness help or hurt a person?

3. Pablita Velarde still works at her art. Think about someone you know who works hard. What keeps this person going?

4. The beautiful landscape around Pablita's home gave her many ideas for her art. Describe a landscape that you think is beautiful.

5. Velarde often did things that women just were not "supposed" to do. What do you think women's and men's roles should be?

UNDERSTANDING WORDS IN CONTEXT

Read the following sentences from the biography. Think about what each underlined word means. In your notebook, write what the word means as it is used in the sentence.

1. Her father was a medicine man, and he treated Pablita [for her loss of sight] with the traditional remedies of his Santa Clara ancestors.

2. Many people thought that she would never see again. Gradually, however, Pablita's sight was restored.

3. She remembers family members using the pigments from the nearby earth to paint colorful designs on the house walls and on the pottery they made.

4. [Dorothy Dunn] also suggested that students use memories of their family and home to inspire them to create their art.

5. [Velarde] was to paint part of a mural that would decorate the wall of a store in Albuquerque, New Mexico.

6. "The calico dresses are . . . patterned with almost <u>mechanical</u> exactness, and the pottery forms are shaped firmly and painted precisely, as in life."

RECALLING DETAILS

1. What two tragic events happened to Pablita when she was 3 years old?

2. When did Velarde decide to become an artist?

3. Choose two people who influenced Velarde and describe their influences on her.

4. Describe Velarde's artwork.

5. What happened in 1948 that was important to Velarde's career?

UNDERSTANDING INFERENCES

In your notebook, write two or three sentences from the biography that support each of the following inferences.

1. Pablita Velarde's use of detail is a very important part of her work.

2. Velarde did not let outside events or the opinions of others keep her from painting.

3. Women artists sometimes have to struggle to succeed.

4. Velarde uses art to keep her family's history and culture alive.

5. When she is troubled, Pablita turns to her heritage for comfort.

INTERPRETING WHAT YOU HAVE READ

1. What effect did losing and then regaining her eyesight have on Velarde?

2. How did growing up in the Rio Grande River valley affect Pablita's work?

3. In what ways was learning under Dorothy Dunn like having Velarde's "sight restored a second time"?

4. In what ways did Tonita Peña serve as a role model for Velarde?

5. Why do you think Velarde created "earth painting"?

ANALYZING QUOTATIONS

Read the following quotation from the biography and answer the questions below.

> *"I sit on my couch and look outside. I have to open lots of little windows in my head—thinking about things that have happened to me, or to someone else that I know. And I remember the stories I heard every winter when I was a girl told by my grandfather or my grandmother, my uncle or father. They are not legends to me. They are real."*

1. What does Velarde mean by "open a lot of little windows in my head"?

2. In what ways are legends, or stories that have been handed down, "real"?

3. How might children's stories still have a powerful meaning for adults?

THINKING CRITICALLY

1. In what positive and negative ways has being a woman affected Velarde's career?

2. Velarde thought, "If [Tonita Peña] can do it, so can I." What does that statement tell you about Velarde?

3. Why do you think Velarde puts so many details into her paintings?

4. How does Velarde's art honor her ancestors, present-day Native Americans, and future generations?

5. Dorothy Dunn was an especially good teacher for Pablita Velarde. Describe a teacher you have had who helped you do your best work.

RODNEY GRANT

Rodney Grant, Omaha actor, played the role of Wind in his
Hair in the Academy Award–winning movie *Dances with Wolves*.
Grant has used his popularity to support the fight against Fetal
Alcohol Syndrome.

Rodney Grant was watching television when the idea flashed into his mind. The movie, *Eagle's Wing*, was about Native Americans. Rodney liked that, yet something was wrong. The main character was a Native American, but the actor playing him was not. At that moment, Grant thought about becoming an actor. He wondered why Native Americans were not acting in movies about their own history. Rodney Grant thought it was time for a change.

It is easy to dream of becoming a movie actor. Actually becoming one is another matter. Very few dreamers, even talented ones, ever make it into the movies. As for Rodney Grant–his chances were slimmer than most people's. He had no acting experience. He did not know anyone in Hollywood, where most movies are made. He could not afford an agent, someone to help him get acting jobs. In addition, Rodney Grant did not fit the Hollywood mold–he is Native American.

Grant did have one important qualification, however–motivation. He knew he wanted to do something of consequence,[1] something that would make him stand out. He remembers, "Everybody else gets married, gets a regular job and sits on the reservation for the rest of their lives. I wanted to be something nobody would expect." Nonetheless, Rodney's decision to become an actor was risky.

Taking risks was nothing new to him, though. Grant, who was born in 1959, faced many difficult, sometimes threatening, situations while growing up on the Omaha Reservation near Winnebago, Nebraska. The Omaha, whose name means "upstream people," once freely traveled the Great Plains. However, like most Native Americans, the Omaha were forced to live on a reservation in the late 1800s. Little by little, European

---

1. consequence (KAHN-sih-kwehns) *n.* importance as a cause or influence

settlers had taken over the land east of the Mississippi River and forced Native Americans to move west. As a "trade" for the lands they had taken, the U.S. government "gave" Native Americans reservations, then forced them to stay within their boundaries.

Reservation life has, for many, created more problems than it has solved. According to Grant, "It's not a pretty life growing up on the reservation. All I saw was death and destruction, a band of people who were struggling to survive." One kind of destruction on the reservation was alcoholism. Grant himself started drinking alcohol when he was 12 years old. Later, his classmates called him the "high school drunk."

Unfortunately, alcoholism is a major cause of death among Native Americans living on reservations today. Alcoholism also contributes to violence, family break-ups, and crime—not only on reservations but in communities all over the United States. Rodney knew, even before he was able to control his alcoholism, that there had to be more to life than drinking. (See **Did You Know?** on page 95 for more information on alcoholism on Native American reservations.)

After Grant left high school, he joined the Marine Corps. He later moved to Lincoln, Nebraska, where he worked at a number of odd jobs. When he was 21 years old, though, Grant took on the biggest job of his life—he began to deal with his alcoholism. He entered a rehabilitation² clinic. There Grant received treatment and counseling for his alcoholism. Eventually, he became a counselor himself, working with other young Native Americans.

During this time Grant saw the movie that made him think about becoming an actor. Having faced his alcoholism, he could now begin to plan a career. But there were other barriers. Rodney explains, "All the Indians I saw in the movies while growing up weren't real Indians. They were every other nationality but Indian: Italian, Mexican." Rodney Grant got his first acting job almost by accident. He was working at night in a

---

2. **rehabilitation** (ree-huh-bihl-uh-TAY-shuhn) *adj.* bringing someone or something back to health

meat-packing plant in Macy, Nebraska. While reading the newspaper during a break, he noticed an advertisement for "extras." Extras are people who appear in movies, usually in crowd scenes. Most often, they do not speak, but they do get paid. Amazingly, the ad called for Native American extras. Rodney did not hesitate, and before long viewers would see him in *We Are One*, a Public Broadcasting System (PBS) program about the lives of Native Americans. His face may have been one among many, but there he was, on TV.

While working for PBS, Grant heard about an audition[3] for a movie called *War Party*. He drove the 500 miles to Tulsa, Oklahoma, to try out. Once again, he got the job. This time Grant had a speaking part, playing the role of Crow Tracker. Because of hard work, and a bit of luck, more acting jobs soon came his way. Finally, it was time for the "big move." In 1989, Grant left for Hollywood, California.

Many famous actors look back on their "big break," the part that leads to better parts–or even to "stardom." When Grant was making *War Party*, he did not know that he was in the middle of his big break. Kevin Costner, a well-known Hollywood actor, was planning a film called *Dances with Wolves* about life on the Great Plains during the late 19th century. Costner insisted on having Native American actors play the more than 250 Native American roles in the film.

Costner had seen Rodney Grant in *War Party*, and he liked what he saw. He called Grant and offered him a starring role. So, after only a few months in Hollywood, Grant's dream was coming true. He, an Omaha, would bring to life the character of a Plains Native American named Wind in His Hair.

Grant says that he identifies with Wind in his Hair. Like the character in the movie, Rodney considers himself skeptical[4] and a bit of a rascal. This "sympathy" for the character may have

---

3. **audition** (aw-DIHSH-uhn) *n.* a test performance to see if an actor, musician, or other performer is suited for a job

4. **skeptical** (SKEHP-tih-kuhl) *adj.* not easily convinced; doubtful

contributed to Grant's ability to make the character seem so real. In any event, *Dances with Wolves* won several Academy Awards, including Best Picture for 1990, and Grant became an "overnight success." Good offers began to flood in, among them a leading role in a TV movie called *Lakota Moon*. Rodney also got a chance to act on stage when he won the role of Story Teller, the narrator, in a ballet called *Winter Moon*.

Although appreciative of the doors Hollywood has opened for him, Grant thinks it is still "business as usual" when it comes to Native American actors. *Dances with Wolves*, in his opinion, is an exception. For the most part, Hollywood continues to cast non-Native Americans in Native American parts. Worse yet, in his view, the movie industry persists[5] in showing white actors in the lead and Native Americans only in supporting roles.

To illustrate, Grant points to the movie *Son of Morning Star*, which tells the story of General Custer. Grant plays the role of Crazy Horse, a famous Oglala warrior who defeated Custer in the famous Battle of Little Bighorn. He says the Native Americans in the film were treated "like extras in the background." The film focuses on Custer. Yet Grant believes that if the facts about the general were presented, Custer would no longer be the hero.

Grant has used his popularity as an actor to support several causes. One of these is the fight against fetal alcohol syndrome (FAS)—a condition that affects the fetus[6] of women who drink during pregnancy. Babies born with FAS can have problems with hearing and seeing as well as with their ability to think and learn. Grant is a spokesperson for the National Organization on FAS because nearly one out of five Native American babies is born with FAS. Also, Grant knows firsthand how dangerous excessive drinking can be.

Rodney Grant continues to act. When he is not acting, he is reading scripts[7] and considering what roles he will take next. He

---

5. **persists** (puhr-SIHSTS) *v.* refuses to give up; continues a certain practice

6. **fetus** (FEET-uhs) *n.* the unborn young of animals and humans

7. **scripts** (SKRIHPTS) *n. pl.* the written text of plays, movies, or TV shows

also takes care of his son, Walter, who Grant says "keeps me centered because I can't forget for one moment that I'm a parent." What if the kinds of roles he wants don't come along? "I'll wash cars or wash dishes or move furniture." Grant would rather act, of course, because as an actor, he says jokingly, "you get paid for working without breaking a sweat. They put water on you if they want you to sweat."

When asked recently how he felt about his heritage, Grant answered, "I'm proud that I'm Native American, but I'm sometimes hurt because other people don't see me as an American citizen as well. As Indians, we try and treat all Americans the same way we'd like to be treated. We wish we could receive that same respect in return. . . . If this is the land of the free and home of the brave, let us treat everybody as such. The possibility for change in America exists; how far that possibility goes is up to each individual. Like the saying goes: If it is to be, it begins with me."

> *Did You Know?* Native American leaders are concerned about the health problems caused by alcoholism in their society. This is not the first time, though, that the health of Native Americans has been seriously threatened. In fact, they began to die almost immediately after Christopher Columbus and his crew landed on an island they named San Salvador (one of what are today called the Bahama Islands). Native Americans had never been exposed to the diseases the explorers carried, so they had not developed immunities, or resistance, to them. Within 40 years, nearly 90 percent of the Native Americans who lived on this island had died from disease. Over the next 400 years, the main cause of death among Native Americans was disease, especially smallpox. Some groups, such as the Mandan, in what is now North Dakota, were almost completely wiped out.

AFTER YOU READ

EXPLORING YOUR RESPONSES

1. Growing up on a reservation was difficult for Rodney Grant. How might you feel if you were forced to live your whole life within the boundaries of your town or city?

2. Grant has worked for causes he believes in. What causes would you work to support?

3. Grant was able to take the unhappy experiences of his youth and turn them into something good. What challenges are common to young people in your town? How can they be overcome?

4. If Rodney had not seen *Eagle's Wing* he might not have decided to become an actor. How much do you think chance influences people's lives? Explain.

5. Grant broke into acting by taking a very small part. Do you think it is better to wait for just what you want or to take whatever comes along as you pursue a goal? Why?

UNDERSTANDING WORDS IN CONTEXT

Read the following sentences from the biography. Think about what each underlined word means. In your notebook, write what the word means as it is used in the sentence.

1. When he was 21 years old, though, Grant . . . entered a rehabilitation clinic. There Grant received treatment and counseling for his alcoholism.

2. While working for PBS, Grant heard about an audition for a movie called *War Party*. He drove 500 miles to Tulsa, Oklahoma, to try out.

3. He knew he wanted to do something of consequence, something that would make him stand out.

4. One of these [causes] is the fight against fetal alcohol syndrome (FAS)–a condition that affects the fetus of women who drink during pregnancy.

5. Rodney Grant continues to act. When he is not acting, he is reading scripts and considering what roles he will take next.

RECALLING DETAILS

1. What did Rodney Grant think was wrong with *Eagle's Wing*?

2. What task did Grant begin at age 21 that would change his life forever?

3. What was the "big break" of Grant's acting career?

4. For what organization is Grant the spokesperson?

5. What does Grant think is wrong with Hollywood?

UNDERSTANDING INFERENCES

In your notebook, write two or three sentences from the biography that support each of the following inferences.

1. Rodney Grant took steps to change his life for the better.

2. Grant did not plan to be an actor.

3. Grant uses his own experiences to help others.

4. People continue to learn even after they leave school.

5. There are different versions of history.

INTERPRETING WHAT YOU HAVE READ

1. In what ways did Rodney Grant's experiences at the rehabilitation clinic eventually help others as well as himself?

2. What do you think Grant means when he says that his son keeps him "centered"?

3. What do you think Grant might have done if he did not become an actor?

4. Why do you think only non–Native Americans played Native American roles in the movies?

5. In what kind of society would Grant like to live?

ANALYZING QUOTATIONS

Read the following quotation from the biography and answer the questions below.

> *"If this is the land of the free and home of the brave, let us treat everybody as such. The possibility for change in America exists; how far that possibility goes is up to each individual. Like the saying goes: If it is to be, it begins with me."*

1. What kind of change is Rodney Grant talking about?

2. Who can bring about this change?

3. In your opinion, what has made or what could make the United States "the land of the free and home of the brave"?

THINKING CRITICALLY

1. In what ways was Rodney Grant's decision to become an actor risky?

2. Do you think actors should only play characters with their cultural background, or should they play any part? Explain.

3. What kind of "destruction" was Grant referring to when talking about reservation life?

4. Why do you think Grant is so concerned about fetal alcohol syndrome?

5. What have you learned about pursuing a goal from Rodney Grant's experience?

JAUNE QUICK-TO-SEE SMITH

Jaune Quick-to-See Smith, Flathead painter, draws upon her experiences to add richness and depth to her artwork. The painting *Storyteller,* shown here, is a pastel collage of realistic and abstract images.

The visitors stood clustered around the painting called *The Spotted Owl*. They studied the three large panels that made up the piece. Vividly painted tree trunks suggested an imaginary forest, where sunlight and shadows danced in and out. Two axes were stuck in the canvas. Finally an observer blurted out, "Where is it? I do not see the owl."

"That's the point," answered the artist.

The owl is not in the painting because the spotted owl is rapidly disappearing from the forests around us. What sort of artist would stick axes in a work of art and title a painting with no owls *The Spotted Owl*? Someone who cares as much about the world around her as she does about creating beautiful images—Jaune (ZHAHN) Quick-to-See Smith.

Such strong visual messages have made Quick-to-See Smith a celebrated[1] artist. Her success comes from her ability to make people think and feel in new ways. Quick-to-See Smith wants to jolt people into seeing problems they can help solve. She also wants them to see, as if for the first time, the beauty in nature and in the Native American culture she knows so well.

Jaune's path to success has been full of twists and turns. Born on the Flathead Reservation in southwestern Montana in 1940, Jaune considers herself very lucky to be here. "By all odds," she says, "I should not be [alive]. . . . When I was born, [only] one in ten Indian children survived." Surviving birth was just the first of many challenges.

One of 11 children, Quick-to-See Smith recalls the difficulties of her early life: "My father was a horse trader; he moved all the time. [He] raised me—I did not have a mother [around]." Whenever possible, Jaune joined her father on long trading trips

---

1. **celebrated** (SEHL-uh-brayt-ihd) *adj.* famous; often talked about

from one reservation to another. At other times, she had to stay with foster families.[2] Poverty added to the problems Jaune faced.

All was not bad, though. Arthur Smith was talented at his work, and he also had a gift for drawing. From her father, Jaune learned to love the land and its creatures. She also learned to draw, and she quickly showed a remarkable ability. Making pictures was doubly rewarding—Jaune could study the things she loved in nature and do something for which she showed a talent.

"As far back as I can remember," Jaune says, "I wanted to be an artist, before I even knew the word. I worked in fields when I was ten as a farm hand, after school, and I used some of that money to send away for the Famous Artists Course,[3] because I knew that's what I was going to be."

Jaune Quick-to-See Smith's struggle to achieve her goal seemed hopeless at times. Her high school advisor did not help her. "I was told very bluntly," Jaune remembers, "that I was not college material." Undaunted,[4] she enrolled in a local junior college, taking as many art courses as the school offered. One day, Jaune's art instructor informed her that, although her drawing was the best in her class, she should reconsider becoming an artist. Such a career was only for men, he told her. Maybe she could teach, he suggested.

"I can't tell you the pain and anguish I felt, because I had worked so long toward this goal. Since I was six I had been thinking about it," Jaune once told an interviewer. Sticking with it, though, she earned an Associate of Arts degree in 1958.

Quick-to-See Smith's drive for further education took her in many directions and to many places. After attending five different colleges, she finally earned a bachelor's degree, graduating with honors from Framingham State College in Massachusetts in

---

2. **foster families** families who care for the children of others on a temporary basis
3. **Famous Artists Course** a course of study offered through the mail that teaches the techniques of well-known artists
4. **undaunted** (un-DAWNT-ihd) *adj.* not discouraged

1974. That same year, Jaune moved to New Mexico. There she completed her master's degree in 1980 at the University of New Mexico. It had taken her 22 years to reach this goal. But during those years, Quick-to-See Smith had married, had three children, held dozens of jobs, and worked at her art.

Her long struggle gave her strength and added richness to her work. "It took a long time, working nights and days, mainly just surviving—so I've been a plugger, and I've kept at it, and it's all right, because the things have come together: the travels, the experiences, have helped the work, made it mature, knowledgeable, work that has a good substance, a foundation to grow on. . . . I've got staying power now," Quick-to-See Smith concludes.

Since the mid-1970s, Jaune has shown her works in galleries and museums all over the country. (See **Did You Know?** on page 104 for more information on Native American art museums.) She is especially known for her various "series." Each series of artwork has a specific name and might include as many as 200 pieces. What these series show is Quick-to-See Smith's love of the land. As she says, "All living things must coexist.[5] . . . The earth does not belong to humankind; humankind belongs to the earth." The series also reflect her diverse heritage. Jaune's roots are a mixture of French and Native American—Cree, Shoshone (shoh-SHOH-nee), and Salish (SAY-lish).

Watching Jaune at work is as interesting as looking at her art. To begin, she might block out large rectangular areas using pastel or earth-colored paint. She might then use charcoal to draw stick figures of hunters, arrows, horses, mountains, or rivers over the soft background. Then she adds real objects, such as hunks of rope, pieces of cloth, newspaper headline clippings, dried flowers—even axes. Quick-to-See Smith uses anything that will help her say what she wants to say in a piece. "In my art . . . I put it all in. It is like a collage,[6] a diary of my life," she says.

---

5. coexist (koh-ihg-ZIHST) *v.* to live together peacefully

6. collage (kuh-LAHZH) *n.* an artwork made up of many different materials

Jaune Quick-to-See Smith's work goes beyond creating art. She uses her leadership skills to help bring together Native American artists. For example, Quick-to-See Smith has organized a group of artists on the Flathead Reservation in Montana, where she goes every year to encourage and teach new talent. At the University of New Mexico in Albuquerque, Jaune has started another group for Native American women artists, called the Grey Canyon Artists. This organization arranges shows of its members' work around the country.

When this group was organized, few women artists, especially Native American women, were finding acceptance. Working together, though, Quick-to-See Smith and the other artists were able to open doors. As time went by, the art community began to take the work of these artists more seriously. Their work was gaining recognition not just because the artists were Native Americans or women, but because their work was fresh and bold.

Since the early 1980s, Quick-to-See Smith also has taught and lectured throughout the United States and in other countries. She sees herself as a "bridge maker" between two artistic and social cultures—the Native American and the European American. She urges people to re-examine the history of the United States so that *both* cultures can understand each other. To spread these ideas, Quick-to-See Smith has put together numerous touring art exhibits. Included in these exhibits are works that celebrate the history and culture of her people.

Quick-to-See Smith believes that things are changing—for the better. "In my half century of life, I've witnessed extreme poverty, poor health care, . . . cultural loss, infant mortality[7] levels that are twice the national average, the highest suicide rates in the U.S., and unemployment as high as 80 percent. But today there is a newly awakened pride and interest in tribal life and a new vitality in our communities. I see energy, determination, conviction, and vision among our tribal peoples."

7. **infant mortality** (mawr-TAL-ih-tee) the death of newborn babies

Quick-to-See Smith's work has been the subject of three documentary[8] films and has received numerous awards. Other people might slow down, take time to enjoy the success, but not Jaune Quick-to-See Smith. "I'm an obsessive[9] worker," she admits.

But obsession is not always enough. "There was a time," the artist recalls, "when I had the obsession, but I did not have vision. I did not have the foundation to have vision. . . . It took twenty years of thinking, moving, and going to school and pulling things together to create the vision." Jaune's grandmother gave her the name Quick-to-See. Perhaps she knew that Jaune had the vision and the gift to bridge two worlds.

> ***Did You Know?*** *The Institute of American Indian Arts, in Santa Fe, New Mexico, was founded by Native Americans to display contemporary Native American art. The museum is the only one of its kind in the world. The president of the institute, Kathryn Harris Tijerina, calls the museum "a setting for our own cultural voice."*

8. **documentary** (dahk-yoo-MEHNT-uh-ree) *adj.* presenting an account of real events

9. **obsessive** (uhb-SEHS-ihv) *adj.* focused on one thing

AFTER YOU READ

EXPLORING YOUR RESPONSES

1. Jaune says, "As far back as I can remember, I wanted to be an artist." Based on what you know about young children, was Jaune's early decision unusual? Explain.

2. The artist was told she was not "college material." What qualities and skills do you think make a person "college material"?

3. Jaune held many different kinds of jobs while she attended school and raised her family. How do you think varied work experience can help a person become a better artist?

4. Smith is very concerned about the environment. Do you think an artist's work should make a statement or should it just picture something? Explain.

5. Jaune sacrificed a great deal to get her education. In your opinion, how valuable is a college degree?

UNDERSTANDING WORDS IN CONTEXT

Read the following sentences from the biography. Think about what each underlined word means. In your notebook, write what the word means as it is used in the sentence.

1. Such strong visual messages have made Quick-to-See Smith a celebrated artist. Her success comes from her ability to make people think and feel in new ways.

2. Whenever possible, Jaune joined her father on long trading trips from one reservation to another. At other times she had to stay with foster families.

3. "I was told very bluntly," Jaune remembers, "that I was not college material." Undaunted, she enrolled in a local junior college.

4. Quick-to-See Smith uses anything that will help her say what she wants to say in a piece. "In my art . . . I put it all in. It is like a collage."

5. Other people might slow down, take time to enjoy the success, but not Jaune Quick-to-See Smith. "I'm an obsessive worker," she admits.

RECALLING DETAILS

1. Why does Jaune consider that she was lucky as an infant?
2. How did Jaune react to her art instructor's advice?
3. How did Quick-to-See Smith get her education?
4. What are some of the ideas and images in Jaune's artwork?
5. How has Quick-to-See Smith expressed her interest in fellow artists?

UNDERSTANDING INFERENCES

In your notebook, write two or three sentences from the biography that support each of the following inferences.

1. Jaune's early life on the reservation was difficult.
2. Quick-to-See Smith has a genuine respect for all living things.
3. For some artists, it takes time to develop a vision—their own imaginative way of looking at the world.
4. Jaune believes the improvements for Native Americans come from within their own communities.
5. Fame has not changed Quick-to-See Smith's commitment to her work.

INTERPRETING WHAT YOU HAVE READ

1. What role did Jaune's love of art play in her childhood?
2. How did Jaune's father influence her as a person and as an artist?

3. Why do you think Jaune's art teacher tried to discourage her?

4. Why do you think Quick-to-See Smith sees a need for people to be "bridges" between Native American and European American cultures?

5. Why do you think Quick-to-See Smith use real objects in her paintings?

ANALYZING QUOTATIONS

Read the following quotation from the biography. Answer the questions that follow.

> *"All living things must coexist. . . . The earth does not belong to humankind; humankind belongs to the earth."*

1. What do you think Quick-to-See Smith means when she says, "All living things must coexist"?

2. How does Quick-to-See Smith's view of the earth reflect her Native American heritage?

3. Do you think the earth "belongs to humankind" or does humankind "belong to the earth"? Explain.

THINKING CRITICALLY

1. Why do you think the land is so important to Jaune?

2. How might Quick-to-See Smith's life have been different if she had listened to her advisor and art teacher?

3. What difficulties might a beginning artist face?

4. How can art create the "bridge" that Jaune wants to build between Native Americans and others?

5. Do you think art can change people's minds? Why or why not?

CULTURAL CONNECTIONS

Thinking About What People Do

1. Choose the person from this unit who you think faced the greatest challenge to achieve his or her goals. Write a paragraph telling why you think that person's struggle was particularly difficult. Give examples.

2. Imagine that you went to school with one of the people in this unit. Write a letter to your "classmate" giving the kind of support and encouragement that will help this person achieve success.

3. Select one of the people in the unit who you think made some good decisions. List the decisions and write two paragraphs describing how that person's life might have been different if he or she had made other choices.

Thinking About Culture

1. All of the people in this unit had to deal with prejudice against Native Americans. Tell how their experiences were similar and how they were different.

2. Imagine that you are a TV reporter doing a story on reservation life. What positive and negative conditions will you film and discuss? You might form a "film crew" with other students on this project.

3. The section titled *Did You Know?* that follows each biography tells you more about the cultural history of the subject and his or her nation. Choose one of the unit subjects and explain how that information helps you understand the subject better.

Building Research Skills

Work with a partner to complete the following activity.

Three of the subjects in this unit are artists. Choose one whose work interests you, using the works pictured on pages 62, 81, and 99 as a guide. Make a list of questions you would like to answer about your artist's work. Your questions might include:

Hint: You may want to check the Bibliography at the back of this book. The Bibliography has a list of books and articles that can help you start your research.

☆ What kind of art does this person create—paintings, photographs, collages, sculptures, or line drawings?

Hint: Look in the card catalog or computer data base of your library for information about the artist's heritage.

☆ Where is the art exhibited?

☆ What materials were used—oil paints, charcoal, or other materials?

Hint: You might want to talk to your art teacher or the curator at a local museum for more information about the artist.

☆ How did the artist's heritage influence his or her work?

Next, go to the library to find out the answers to your questions.

Present your findings to the class in the form of an oral report. If possible, display examples of the artist's work.

Extending Your Studies

MATH **Your task:** *To calculate winning speeds.* In the 1964 Olympics, Billy Mills ran the 10,000-meter run in a little more than 28 minutes. How fast did he run? To find out, convert the distance he traveled into kilometers, then into miles. Ten thousand meters is 10 kilometers, which is about 6 miles. So, Billy Mills traveled 6 miles in 28 minutes. If he kept going at this same rate, how many miles would he travel in an hour? Use this formula:

$$\frac{6 \ (\text{miles})}{28 \ (\text{minutes})} = \frac{x \ (\text{miles})}{60 \ (\text{minutes})}$$

To finish the equation: $28x = 360$; $x = 360/28$; $x = 12.85$.
Billy Mills was traveling 12.85 miles per hour!

Use this procedure to calculate these winning speeds:

☆ Secretariat, a famous racehorse, ran 1.25 miles in just under 2 minutes in the 1973 Kentucky Derby. How many miles per hour did she run? (*Hint*: Begin with this equation: $1.25/2 = x/60$)

☆ In 1980, speed skater Eric Heiden broke an Olympic record when he skated 5,000 meters in a little more than 7 minutes. How fast did he skate? (*Hint*: 5,000 meters is about 3 miles.)

☆ Swimmer Janet Evans broke a world record in 1988 when she swam 1,500 meters in just under 16 minutes. How fast did she swim? (*Hint*: 1,500 meters is about 1 mile.)

HEALTH **Your task:** *To create a directory of resources for chemically dependent people in your community.* You read that Rodney Grant has been a spokesperson for fetal alcohol syndrome. Grant knows that the first step in a person's recovery from substance abuse is asking for help. Yet many people may not know whom to ask.

As a class, create a directory of services that are available in your community to assist chemically dependent people and their families. Here are some places to begin your research:

☆ The Yellow Pages of the telephone directory (look for Substance Abuse Counseling)

☆ The white pages of the telephone directory (look for drug hotlines, Alcoholics Anonymous, Narcotics Anonymous, Alanon, and Alateen)

☆ The community section of your newspaper (look for local organizations)

☆ School counselors, doctors, clergy members, and police departments

Arrange your directory in alphabetical order, then type and copy it. Local businesses might sponsor your efforts through donations or allow you to place free copies in their stores.

VISUAL ARTS **Your task:** *To create a collage that carries a message.* In this unit, you read about Jaune Quick-to-See Smith's painting *The Spotted Owl*. This painting includes two real axes stuck into the canvas. These axes carry Quick-to-See Smith's message: The spotted owl is vanishing because people are chopping down the trees in which the owl makes its home.

Create a collage that expresses a message that you would like to tell the world. A collage is an artwork that may include pictures, news headlines, or found objects, including paper clips, telephone wire, stones, or other items. Select one object to be the focus of your collage, then choose the others to make your message clearer. Decide on a title for your collage and display it in the classroom.

WRITING WORKSHOP

As you know, a biography is the true story of a person's life. In this lesson, you will write a **biographical sketch of someone you know**–a classmate or someone about your own age. Since your biography will be a "sketch" of the person you choose, do not try to cover the person's entire life. Just think about an event or a situation that shows what this person is like. Then write your sketch to introduce your subject to the class.

PREWRITING

Begin your biographical sketch by selecting a friend or classmate whom you know well and with whom you have shared some experience. Before you make your decision, though, review what you know about the person and the details of the experience you shared. Think about what happened and what both of you did and said. Make sure you have a clear picture of the person and experience so that you will be able to make the scene come alive for your reader. You might want to choose two or three possible subjects first, then narrow your search.

Before you select a subject, decide which person and experience you remember best and which you can describe best for your reader.

Once you are sure of your subject and the experience you will discuss, you can begin your prewriting activities. Here are two suggestions to get started:

Brainstorming: You may know which person and event you want to write about, but be unsure of how to begin. Brainstorming is one way to explore your topic. Think about your subject, and on a blank sheet of paper, write any word or phrase that comes to mind. Explore words that describe the person's character, appearance, habits, hobbies, and sense of humor. Use details that appeal to the senses.

As you brainstorm, include ideas or events that concern your subject. Think about how you know the person, for example, or when and where you met. Your brainstorming notes may look something like this:

Thoughts About Jeff

met Jeff in the cafeteria
red hair
big grin
shy around girls
likes to bike
family is from Texas

always bumping into things
can laugh at himself
tried out for the class play
writes for school newspaper
generous, friendly
led the food drive

Freewriting: Look at the words and ideas you brainstormed. Choose one that seems to jump out at you and begin writing. Do not think too much about what you write, just write freely for two minutes. Your freewriting will help you create a word sketch of your subject.

Organize: Think about how you can use your brainstorming notes and the ideas or event you explored in your freewriting. Arrange your ideas so that they show the real person—what he or she is like as a person, not just his or her outward appearance.

DRAFTING

Now you can begin *drafting* your biographical sketch. Use the following strategies to help you begin:

Use specific language: Choose words that help your reader see and understand your subject. For example, read the following sentences. Which one gives you a clear picture of Morgan?

Morgan has a nice smile.

Morgan's smile lights up her whole face.

What pictures do you see in your mind after you read both sentences? A "nice smile" does not give you much detail, so it is difficult to get an exact picture of Morgan. A smile that "lights up her whole face," though, probably makes you think of a very happy person with a big grin and smiling eyes. The second sentence, then, gives you enough detail to allow you to construct a mental picture of Morgan.

As you draft your biographical sketch, use as much specific language as you can so that your reader can "see" your subject.

Now you are ready to write your draft. At this point, do not worry about word usage and spelling errors. Concentrate on getting your ideas down on paper in a clear, understandable way. You will check for errors when you proofread your work.

REVISING

Put your sketch aside for a day or two. Then, with the help of another student who will act as your editor, evaluate and **revise** your work. See the directions for writers and student editors below.

Directions for Writers: Read your work aloud, listening to how it flows. Then ask yourself these questions:

☆ Does my opening hold the reader's attention?

☆ Am I *showing,* not *telling,* what happened?

☆ Did I include interesting details?

☆ Does my description make my subject come alive?

Make notes for your next draft or revise your work before you give it to a student editor. Then, ask the student editor to read your work. Listen carefully to his or her suggestions. If they seem helpful, use them to improve your writing when you revise your work.

Directions for Student Editors: Read the work carefully and respectfully, remembering that your purpose is to help the writer do his or her best work. Keep in mind that an editor should always make positive, helpful comments that point to specific parts of the essay. After you read the work, use the following questions to help you direct your comments:

☆ What do I like most about this biographical sketch?

☆ Can I see the person or event in my mind?

☆ Do I feel I know the subject?

☆ Has the writer used details to describe the subject?

☆ What did the writer learn about his or her subject?

PROOFREADING

When you are satisfied that your work says what you want it to say, check it carefully for errors in spelling, punctuation, capitalization, and grammar. Then make a neat, final copy of your biographical sketch.

PUBLISHING

After you have revised your writing, you are ready to publish or share it. Put together a classroom portrait gallery called Someone You Should Know, and display the sketches for everyone to read.

NATIVE AMERICANS IN SCIENCE AND ENGINEERING

In this unit you will read about five Native Americans who have left their mark in the sciences and engineering. As you read, think about some of the personal qualities and challenges that they have in common. Think, too, about what makes each person special.

Rocket-design engineer **Mary Ross**, a Cherokee, blazed many trails. "I didn't mind being the only girl in my math class," she says. "Math, chemistry, and physics were more fun."

Al Qöyawayma (koo-YAH-weye-mah) is a Hopi mechanical engineer and a talented potter. Of his pottery making he writes, "[Because] I know that some of this clay may even contain the dust of my ancestors . . . how respectful I must be."

Mohawk environmental engineer **Laura Weber** urges people to care about the environment. She says, "Indian tradition teaches us that we should respect and love the Earth as we would our mother."

His Navajo heritage made physicist **Fred Begay** (buh-GAY) curious about how the world works. As he explains, "A scientist looks at the world as a child does, always wondering, . . . What are the pieces of the pieces of the pieces?"

"Preparing for a health career requires dedication and hard work," says **Dr. Lois Steele**, an Assiniboine (uh-SIHN-uh-boyn), "but achieving any worthwhile goal in life usually does."

As you read the unit, think about how each person's experiences contributed to his or her career choice. You might be surprised at the number of similarities in these areas.

MARY ROSS

Mary Ross, Cherokee engineer, displays her rocket designs. Because women have always been valued members of Cherokee society, Ross was confident that she could succeed in a field dominated by men.

The object of the 1950s TV game show *What's My Line?* was to guess what the "mystery guest" did for a living. The panelists,[1] who were celebrities, would ask the mystery guest questions to try to guess his or her occupation. To make the show intriguing,[2] the person's occupation was unusual—everything from hunting underwater treasure to designing clothes for pets.

One week in 1958, a woman named Mary Ross was the mystery guest. The panelists were not easily stumped[3]—they had lots of experience with women. Was she a special kind of teacher? Did she write strange stories? Was she a model, perhaps? After asking many questions, however, they could not guess what her job was. The funny thing is, Mary Ross's job was not so unusual. In fact, it was rather common—thousands of people did what Mary did. But it never occurred to the panelists of *What's My Line?* that a woman would design missiles and rockets.

Mary Ross probably was not too surprised that she "fooled" the TV panel. She was used to people's disbelief when she told them she was an advanced systems engineer. For most of her life, Ross did things that most women did not do. To become a rocket-design engineer in the 1940s, she had to break down quite a few barriers. Mary was confident, though, that she could make it because she had been raised in a society that values and supports women—the Cherokee society. (See **Did You Know?** on page 122 for more information on Ross's Cherokee heritage.)

Long before women in the United States were allowed to vote, Cherokee women sat on tribal councils—the basis of

---

1. **panelists** (PAN-uhl-ihsts) *n. pl.* a group of people gathered to judge, discuss, or ask questions
2. **intriguing** (ihn-TREEG-ihng) *adj.* fascinating; interesting
3. **stumped** (STUMPT) *adj.* puzzled; confused

Cherokee government. Men and women shared the responsibility for making important decisions. Mary learned that being female did not limit her choices.

Still, Mary Ross, who was born in 1908, grew up in a world different from the one we know today—especially for women. Until the 1960s, women in the United States rarely worked outside the home after they married. Some women went to college, but not usually to prepare for a profession. It was rare for a woman to study mathematics or science. The assumption[4] was that men were more successful in these areas than women were, and few people questioned this assumption. Not Mary Ross. "I didn't mind being the only girl in my math class. Math, chemistry, and physics were more fun to study than any other subjects," she recalls. Mary graduated from high school when she was 16 years old—full of love for what were considered "boys' subjects."

After high school, Mary Ross decided to continue studying math and science in college. By 1928, she had earned a degree from Northeastern State University in Tahlequah, Oklahoma. For eight years, Ross taught math and science in a public high school. But she wanted to do even more. Beginning in 1938, Mary started skipping vacations in summer and going to school instead. Four years later, she had a master's degree in mathematics, a specialty that would soon be in demand.

In the early 1940s, the United States was at war, and was feverishly building aircraft—planes, jets, and rockets. The world was alarmed by Adolf Hitler's rise to power in Germany. Increasingly, people in the United States were realizing that they would have to stop him. Aircraft companies began searching for engineers to help build a new air force.

In 1941, Ross visited friends in southern California, where many large aircraft companies were located. During her visit, she applied for and got a job with Lockheed, a leading aircraft

---

4. **assumption** (uh-SUMP-shuhn) *n.* anything taken for granted

company. There, her employers decided she could become an engineer. Engineers apply mathematics in their work. Mary was qualified—and determined. It was time to break down the barrier between women and careers in engineering. Mary Ross, by the way, was the first woman engineer that Lockheed ever employed.

Confident as she was, Ross still had a lot to learn—not so much about engineering as about managing a career. She remembers, "I was naive[5] and didn't know the first thing about how to negotiate[6] for a job or for salary." But she quickly learned. At first, Ross worked as an assistant to another mathematician. In a few years, however, she was doing her own research, and other engineers were working for her. She soon joined a group of 40 other engineers to design guided missiles—rockets that can fly by themselves and find targets with pinpoint accuracy.

Later she helped design both manned and unmanned earth-orbiting vehicles, lunar landers, and deep space probes. Among the unmanned earth-orbiting vehicles that we use every day are weather and communications satellites. Weather satellites warn us of storms, so people can take action to save lives and property. Communications satellites help people stay in contact by telephone and television with events around the world.

Ross worked on other programs, too. The Mercury, Gemini, and Apollo programs allowed astronauts to travel safely to and from the moon. In addition, the Mariner, Pioneer, and Voyager programs allowed us to send fly-bys past all of the planets, except Pluto. These vehicles send back to Earth information and pictures that greatly increase our knowledge of the universe.

Mary Ross has retired from her job as an engineer, but she is still an active member of the Society of Women Engineers, an organization that supports women engineers and encourages young women to study engineering. To honor all that Ross has

---

5. **naive** (nah-EEV) *adj.* innocent; unaware

6. **negotiate** (nih-GOH-shee-ayt) *v.* to discuss and come to an agreement

achieved, the society has established an engineering scholarship in her name.

Throughout her career, Ross has received many honors and awards. But perhaps her greatest reward has been knowing that she has cleared the path for other women. In 1978, Sally Ride became the first female U.S. astronaut to travel into space. Before Ride could make her historic trip into space, however, engineers like Ross had to design the spaceship and plan the journey. In many ways, Ross has been a pioneer—someone who has the bravery and strength to be the first at something, so that others can follow in her footsteps. It is because of people like Mary Ross that women engineers will no longer stump panelists on programs like *What's My Line?*

> **Did You Know?** *Mary Ross's great-great-grandfather, John Ross, is a famous figure in Cherokee as well as U.S. history. As chief of the Cherokee nation for almost 40 years, he devoted his life to the education and progress of his people. John Ross so loved learning that he built his own library. When he died in 1866, the Cherokee recognized him as "a friend of education" who "faithfully encouraged schools throughout the country."*

AFTER YOU READ

EXPLORING YOUR RESPONSES

1. Mary Ross grew up in a community that valued education. How might her life have been different if she had had to struggle for an education?

2. In a way, Ross was a pioneer. Describe someone you think of as a pioneer. Explain his or her importance to you.

3. Ross felt there were many things she did not know about working when she started her first job. What skills and attitudes do you think people need to succeed in a job?

4. For many years engineering was considered a "man's" job. Think of a job you would like to do. Was it once considered a "man's" job or a "woman's" job? Why do you think this was so?

5. Mary Ross was involved in an exciting engineering project—space flight. If you could be involved in an exciting project in any field, what would it be? Explain.

UNDERSTANDING WORDS IN CONTEXT

Read the following sentences from the biography. Think about what each underlined word means. In your notebook, write what the word means as it is used in the sentence.

1. The panelists, who were celebrities, would ask the mystery guest questions to try to guess his or her occupation.

2. To make the show intriguing, the person's occupation was unusual—everything from hunting underwater treasure to designing clothes for pets.

3. The panelists were not easily stumped—they had lots of experience.

4. It was rare for a woman to study mathematics or science. The <u>assumption</u> was that men were more successful in these areas than women were.

5. "I . . . didn't know the first thing about how to <u>negotiate</u> for a job or for salary."

RECALLING DETAILS

1. When did Mary Ross grow up?
2. What school subjects did Ross like as a girl?
3. Why did Mary Ross stump the panelists on *What's My Line?*
4. Name some of the engineering projects Ross worked on.
5. How has Mary Ross helped other women engineers?

UNDERSTANDING INFERENCES

In your notebook, write two or three sentences from the biography that support each of the following inferences.

1. The Cherokee have a history of treating women and men equally.
2. The Cherokee place a high value on education.
3. Mary Ross was willing to work hard to achieve her goals.
4. Assumptions about what people can and cannot do can be mistaken.
5. Ross's job as an engineer was exciting and challenging.

INTERPRETING WHAT YOU HAVE READ

1. Mary Ross grew up in a community that valued learning. How does her life reflect this attitude about education?
2. Women in Cherokee society traditionally had power. How might this tradition have affected Mary Ross's career?
3. How did Ross's skill in mathematics help her in engineering?

4. Ross said that she did not know how to negotiate a salary. How might this have affected her?

5. How are people today benefiting from Ross's knowledge and experiences?

ANALYZING QUOTATIONS

Read the following quotation from the biography and answer the questions below.

> *Perhaps [Ross's] greatest reward has been knowing that she has cleared the path for other women.*

1. In what way did Mary Ross "clear the path for other women"?

2. Whose work do you think is more important: the person who clears the path or the person who walks the path to success? Explain.

3. Think of someone you know who has a goal. What might you do "behind the scenes" to help that person achieve his or her goal?

THINKING CRITICALLY

1. Why do you think women were not encouraged to go into math and science?

2. In what ways could Mary Ross be considered a "pioneer"?

3. In what ways does Ross's life carry on the traditions of her great-great grandfather John Ross and the Cherokee nation?

4. What do you think is Mary Ross's greatest achievement? Explain.

5. Think about ways in which you have been or might be a pioneer. Describe what being a pioneer means to you.

AL QÖYAWAYMA

Al Qöyawayma, Hopi mechanical engineer, conducts a river field survey. His concern for the environment and his interest in traditional Hopi pottery making reflect Qöyawayma's pride in his heritage.

If Al Qöyawayma (koh-YAH-weye-mah) had a time machine, he would set the dial for about the year 1400. He would go back to a time when pottery making flourished[1] among his Hopi ancestors. Even though, as a mechanical engineer, Al is very much a part of the 20th century, as a potter, he is part of a timeless tradition. Once he arrived in the year 1400, he says, "I wouldn't be out of place. There might be a bit of cultural shock. But I don't think I would be lost." Qöyawayma never seems lost—whether he is on the telephone talking to someone in Washington, D.C., about the environmental impact of a proposed power plant or sitting alone thinking about the shape of a piece of pottery he is working on.

Living at ease in two different worlds is nothing new for Qöyawayma. Born in 1938 in Los Angeles, California, he was raised to succeed in U.S. society but never to forget his Hopi heritage. Al's parents had moved to Los Angeles in the 1930s from their home on the Hopi reservation in northeastern Arizona. When they arrived, there were already many Hopi living in the city. In fact, there are more Hopi in Los Angeles than anywhere else, except the reservation.

At the turn of the century, there was an exodus[2] of Hopi people to California. At that time, the U.S. government was encouraging Native Americans to leave their reservations. Officials believed that living "off-reservation" would help Native Americans assimilate[3] better into "mainstream" life. Some Hopi assimilated very well—even to the point of changing their Hopi

---

1. **flourished** (FLER-ihsht) *v.* grew and developed strongly
2. **exodus** (EHKS-uh-duhs) *n.* the departure of many people
3. **assimilate** (uh-SIHM-uh-layt) *v.* to become like others

names to English names. Al's parents chose to live in both worlds, rather than trade one for the other.

After graduating from high school, Qöyawayma went to the California State Polytechnical University at San Luis Obispo (oh-BIHS-poh). There he earned a degree in mechanical engineering. Mechanical engineers design and build bridges, engines, and machines. Some people think it is a demanding course of study, and a demanding career. But Al found it easy. He went on to earn a master's degree in control systems engineering from the University of California in 1966.

After graduate school, Al worked for a Los Angeles company designing aircraft equipment. He was very successful, and several of his inventions are patented. This means that he legally "owns" the inventions, and no one can make them without his permission or without paying for the right to make them. Throughout all this time, however, Qöyawayma knew that something just was not right. Though a well-respected professional, he did not feel fulfilled. Al felt a strong pull to return to the beautiful mesas[4] of his ancestors.

In 1971, Al Qöyawayma's opportunity arrived. He was offered an important job with the Salt River Project (SRP) in Arizona. The SRP is a utility company that provides power and water to people who live in the central part of the state. Al took the job for a number of reasons. He could help protect the environment, and he could create a department of very talented engineers and scientists. Perhaps the most important reason, though, was knowing that he would be closer to the Hopi and other Arizona Native Americans. "My work [in Los Angeles] didn't have any interaction with Indian tribes. I wanted to get closer to home, to do things I could apply to the social sense of working with our people."

As Manager of Environmental Services, Qöyawayma's job at the SRP is to make sure that the company does not pollute the environment. When the SRP wants to build something or use

4. **mesas** (MAY-suhz) *n. pl.* flat-topped mountains with steep sides

certain fuels to make energy, Al and his staff figure out what impact these changes will have on the environment. He is concerned not only about the health effects of what the SRP does. Al tries to protect the beauty of the land and air, too. Known as a perfectionist,[5] he sets high standards for the people and programs he manages.

Qöyawayma also helps his company find new sources of water. Frequently, this water is located on land owned by Native Americans. As a result, Al's job can be very difficult at times. Sometimes the interests of the utility company go against the needs of Native American communities. For example, the utility company wants to build dams in central Arizona. The dams, however, would flood Native American land. Al's job is to balance these conflicting needs. He explains, "The closer you get to your homeland where it has resources in conflict with people who are using them, water rights become conflict, land is conflict, everything is conflict. . . . I contributed in bringing our own SRP management, the government, and tribal leaders together to look at the conflict and resolve it. . . . I didn't need to be present. . . . But I was there, and I think I made a difference."

One day, while visiting his aunt, who lived in New Oraibi (ohr-EYEV-ee) on the Hopi reservation, he learned to make pottery the Hopi way. At first, he just helped his aunt. When the time was right, though, she asked him, "Well, why don't you try some?" This simple question changed his life. "It was after I really collected the materials [for making pottery] and decided I was really going to concentrate. Then the real, real interesting creative feelings came to me. I was there by myself doing. Nobody else was helping me. You couldn't ask anybody else a question. It was pretty amazing actually."

Qöyawayma was born into an artistic family. His aunt, who died at age 99, was a famous potter. Al's father was a painter for

---

5. **perfectionist** (per-FEHK-shuhn-ihst) *n.* a person who strives to make things perfect

Walt Disney Productions in Los Angeles, and two uncles were also painters. Al himself had tried making pottery in high school, but it was not until his aunt taught him the ancient Sikyatki (see-KEEAHT-kee) method that his talent became obvious. (See **Did You Know?** on page 131 for more information on Sikyatki pottery.)

This method takes a great deal of time and effort. First, Qöyawayma searches the mesas for just the right clay–the same clay his ancestors used 800-1,000 years ago. Next, he breaks up the hard, rocky clay, then strains and sifts it. Al soaks what is left in a strainer in water until the clay becomes a certain consistency[6]–not too wet, not too dry.

To make a pot, he uses the "coil and pull" method. After rolling the clay into coils, Qöyawayma builds a form by placing coils on top of one another. He then smoothes the coils into the shape and thickness he wants. Often, Al finishes a pot by etching in figures, such as ears of corn, which seem to "sprout" from the clay itself. Finally, the pottery is kiln-fired[7] to harden it and to bring out the soft desert colors. Of the whole process, Al says, "It's control. It's patience. And to a large degree it's a feel technique. You can see, but you can also feel. A lot of the time you don't even look; you just feel." According to Qöyawayma, making pottery is as challenging as anything an engineer does. In fact, there are similarities between the two. Engineers test the limits of the materials they work with–and so do potters. Al has made pots with walls so thin that people find it hard to believe they are handmade. Once, the judges rejected a piece that Al had entered in a contest because the clay wall was so fine. They thought it had been made by a machine.

Qöyawayma has yet another side. He is one of the founders of the American Indian Science and Engineering Society (AISES).

6. **consistency** (kuhn-SIHS-tuhn-see) *n.* the texture and weight of something neither solid nor liquid

7. **kiln-fired** (KIHL-FEYERD) *adj.* baked at a very high temperature in a kiln oven

AISES is an organization that helps Native Americans become scientists and engineers. One of Al's favorite projects is organizing chapters, or local branches, of AISES in high schools and colleges. His own staff—which includes two Navajos and one Zuni—reflects his commitment to training highly qualified Native Americans in these fields.

In Al Qöyawayma, the past and the future, the artist and the scientist are balanced. He writes in a poem, "[Because] I know that some of this clay may even contain the dust of my ancestors . . . how respectful I must be." Qöyawayma continues to use his understanding of the needs of people and the land to solve environmental, and artistic, problems.

> **Did You Know?** There are about 6,000 Hopi who now live on several neighboring mesas in northeastern Arizona. Sikyatki, which means "Yellow House" in English, is an abandoned pueblo. The people who once lived there made fine, beautiful pottery, which dates to the 1400s. These ancient Hopi, along with other Native American groups, had discovered that clay pots were better than baskets or other containers for storing and cooking food. As their society changed, their pottery did, too. The people of Sikyatki created pottery that was artistic as well as useful. The pottery even became part of their religion. Many of the pieces that have survived were found in burial sites. Qöyawayma makes his pottery in almost exactly the same way as the vanished people of Sikyatki.

AFTER YOU READ

EXPLORING YOUR RESPONSES

1. Qöyawayma sometimes must balance the needs of the utility company with the needs of Native Americans. Describe a time when you resolved a conflict.

2. Qöyawayma does not take short cuts—either as an engineer or as a potter. What are the advantages and disadvantages of working in this manner?

3. Connecting with the past is very important to Qöyawayma. Why might it be important to make this connection?

4. Qöyawayma is a talented engineer and a talented potter. How do both activities benefit society?

5. Al Qöyawayma has been very successful at two careers. If you could also be successful at two careers, what careers would you choose? Explain.

UNDERSTANDING WORDS IN CONTEXT

Read the following sentences from the biography. Think about what each underlined word means. In your notebook, write what the word means as it is used in the sentence.

1. At the turn of the century, there was an exodus of Hopi people to California. At that time, the U.S. government was encouraging Native Americans to leave their reservations.

2. Officials believed that living "off-reservation" would help Native Americans assimilate better into "mainstream" life.

3. Known as a perfectionist, [Qöyawayma] sets high standards for the people and programs he manages.

4. Al soaks what is left in a strainer in water until the clay becomes a certain consistency—not too wet, not too dry.

5. Finally, the pottery is kiln-fired to harden it and to bring out the soft desert colors.

RECALLING DETAILS

1. In what two places in the United States do most Hopi live today?

2. What was Al's childhood like?

3. What is the Salt River Project?

4. How does Qöyawayma help young Native Americans become scientists and engineers?

5. How does Al go about making a piece of pottery?

UNDERSTANDING INFERENCES

In your notebook, write two or three sentences from the biography that support each of the following inferences.

1. When it comes to the environment, people can have different ideas about what is right.

2. As a pottery maker, Qöyawayma follows the traditions of his ancestors.

3. Qöyawayma is a talented potter.

4. Qöyawayma thinks engineering is a good career for Native Americans.

5. Some jobs require balancing different needs.

INTERPRETING WHAT YOU HAVE READ

1. Qöyawayma says he "would not be lost" if he found himself among the Hopi pottery makers of the 1400s. Why do you think he would feel comfortable?

2. In what ways did Qöyawayma's upbringing in Los Angeles prepare him for his later success in two careers?

3. How does Qöyawayma's engineering background come out in his pottery?

4. Why do you think Qöyawayma finds it satisfying to work on Native American issues?

5. Why do you think the environment is the source of conflict among people?

ANALYZING QUOTATIONS

Read the following quotation from the biography and answer the questions below.

> *"The closer you get to your homeland where it has resources in conflict with people who are using them, water rights become conflict, land is conflict, everything is conflict. . . . I contributed in bringing our own SRP management, the government, and tribal leaders together to look at the conflict and resolve it."*

1. What role does Al play in resolving land and water conflicts?
2. Why is it important for Native Americans and the government to work together on land and water issues?
3. What aspects of Qöyawayma's career might you find satisfying?

THINKING CRITICALLY

1. What problems might the Hopi who went to Los Angeles in the early 1900s have faced when they tried to blend into U.S. society?
2. Why do you think some Hopis changed their names to English names after they left the reservation?
3. Do you think Qöyawayma would feel fulfilled if he only made pottery? Explain.
4. Qöyawayma respects the clay he uses to make his pottery. Why do you think this is so?
5. Helping people resolve conflicts gives Al Qöyawayma a feeling of satisfaction. What could you do to help others?

LAURA WEBER

Laura Weber, Mohawk environmental engineer, helps companies and communities reduce the amount of waste they produce. Weber believes that her environmental concerns grew out of her Mohawk heritage.

Imagine a football field piled high with trash–91.3 miles high. This huge mountain represents the average amount of waste the United States puts into landfills[1] every year. As an environmental engineer, it is Laura Weber's job to dispose of this waste safely. She also helps companies and communities reduce the amount of waste they produce, which, in turn, helps to protect the environment. Protecting the Earth is not just something Laura learned to care about in school. She believes that her concern grows out of her Mohawk heritage. Like other Native American groups, the Mohawk see the environment and people as interdependent[2]–they need each other for survival.

Laura Weber was born in 1961, in Alexandria Bay, New York. She does not know many details about her background because, says Weber, "My family did not keep track of their tribal heritage because back in those days they were ashamed of it, plus the records weren't kept up to date like they are now." But it was not until college that she re-connected with that heritage and, at the same time, found her path in life.

When Laura entered the University of New York at Plattsburgh, she did not have a career in mind. But before long, a teacher named Veronica Cunningham opened her eyes to a field she had never considered before. Laura remembers, "She was my lab instructor at Plattsburgh my sophomore year. She really sparked the interest. It was just something that happened. A light switch came on." That light switch was chemistry–the study of what different substances are made of and what happens when they interact.[3] Chemists often search for ways to improve

---

1. **landfills** *n. pl.* areas set aside for garbage
2. **interdependent** (ihn-tuhr-dee-PEHN-duhnt) *adj.* connected by mutual need
3. **interact** (ihn-tuhr-AKT) *v.* to act on one another

people's lives—for instance, by curing diseases or developing no-wrinkle fabrics. Laura Weber liked that, although she was surprised. "When I was in high school I absolutely hated chemistry. If you told me when I was in high school that I would get a degree in chemistry I would have told you you were off your rocker."

Weber wanted more than just a degree in chemistry, however. She realized that to have an influence on the environment, she would also need a degree in engineering, the field that puts the discoveries of science to practical[4] use. Engineers plan, build, and operate things useful in everyday life, such as buildings, roads, and waste disposal systems.

Laura eventually earned two bachelor's degrees, one in chemistry and one in chemical engineering. But Laura's grades were not good enough for her to be accepted as a "regular" graduate student in engineering. So, she was admitted on a trial basis. She would have to prove herself. After the first six months, Laura did just that, with almost a straight-A average. Weber explains, "It was motivation. And all my life I had all these people telling me I couldn't do these things, and I wanted to prove to them that I could."

In 1991, she earned a master's degree in civil and environmental engineering. Weber now had the academic credentials[5] she needed to get to work on the environment.

While still in college, though, something else happened that would mean as much as her degrees. A school counselor found out about Laura's Mohawk ancestry and encouraged her to join the American Indian Society of Engineers and Scientists (AISES). This organization helps Native Americans enter the fields of science and engineering.

Her curiosity aroused, Weber attended an AISES meeting in Seattle, Washington. This meeting changed her life. "There were

---

4. **practical** (PRAK-tih-kuhl) *adj.* workable; of everyday use
5. **credentials** (krih-DEHN-shuhlz) *n. pl.* proof of a person's learning or experience

five- or six hundred people there but we all felt like a family. It really touched me. I came back inspired to do more and get more involved. I became president of the student chapter, organized a Northeast AISES Regional Conference. . . . I connected with my heritage through that conference–the powwow, listening to people talk." (See **Did You Know?** on page 140 for more information on powwows.)

Only a few months after graduating, Laura Weber put her chemistry and engineering degrees together with her renewed interest in her heritage to start a company called Preserve Mother Earth, or PM Earth for short. Laura chose this name carefully. The term *Mother Earth* reflects the Native American belief that people should respect and love the Earth just as they respect and love their mother. The logo[6] for Laura's company is a turtle with a picture of North America on its back. The turtle is a Native American symbol for nature. As the tradition goes, a healthy turtle means that nature is healthy, too. A sick turtle means that nature is in trouble.

PM Earth is based on the idea that the best way to solve a problem is not to create one in the first place. She helps companies look for ways to generate[7] less waste. Weber thinks of her firm as an environmental consulting firm.[8] Her clients learn, for example, how to recycle and how to package products in ways that produce less waste.

PM Earth helps businesses and communities develop their own recycling programs. First, Weber makes clients aware that in 1990, about 180 million tons of solid waste (that 91-mile-high mountain) were created in the United States. Then, she shows the client ways to reduce its share of this gigantic heap. Weber believes that if everyone were to follow the waste management

---

6. **logo** (LOH-goh) *n.* a picture or symbol that is associated with a person or business

7. **generate** (JEHN-uh-rayt) *v.* to cause to be; to produce

8. **consulting firm** a business that offers advice and recommendations

suggestions of companies like PM Earth, we could reduce this mountain of waste to one-tenth of this size.

When Weber helps a client, she looks at three things: reducing the amount of waste, reusing materials, and recycling. She calls these waste management areas the "three Rs." If everyone in the country lived by the three Rs, Laura would have very little business. But for her, that would mean success, not failure. Weber is as much concerned with educating people about their relationship to the environment as with making a profit.

Weber's first opportunity to put her training and beliefs to work was in her own community. She remembers, "In Jefferson County, where my office is located, there is a solid waste management department. I got the names of the people in Jefferson County and simply wrote them a letter saying that I was starting my business, what I specializing in, and my availability for working. A day later, after I had sent the letter out, a person from Jefferson County called me saying they had been looking for somebody with my qualifications."

For the next four months, Laura visited businesses in Jefferson County to evaluate how they disposed of waste. When she finished, Weber made recommendations about reducing waste and setting up recycling programs. She gave the county a complete picture of what was being done and what could be done differently or better.

Starting a business is not easy. For one thing, it takes "luck"–being in the right place at the right time. But more than luck is involved. Weber explains, "The second thing it takes to start your own business is to believe in yourself. When I was in high school and started to tell people I wanted to go to college, they said, 'you'll never make it in college.' I had mediocre[9] grades. People were not confident that I could go to college and be successful. And that was the whole story through my entire

9. **mediocre** (mee-dee-OH-kuhr) *adj.* neither very good nor very bad

time in college, even at Plattsburgh. Even my advisor at Plattsburgh said he didn't know what my chances were."

For Weber, believing in herself includes fulfilling her responsibilities as a Native American. "Indian tradition teaches us that we should respect and love the Earth as we would our mother. Too often, though, we find that people abuse our Mother Earth by improperly using her natural materials and carelessly disposing of wastes which harm the environment." Through PM Earth, Laura Weber will work to show people how to take care of the environment.

> *Did You Know?* *When Laura Weber was a senior in college, she attended a powwow organized by the American Indian Society of Engineers and Scientists (AISES). A powwow is a special meeting of Native Americans, which can be social or serious. At one time, powwows were ceremonies in which people prayed and danced for such things as the health of a sick person, success in hunting or fishing, and a good harvest. Dancing is still a major focus at today's powwows, but the emphasis is a bit different from the powwows of the past. The emphasis now is on helping Native Americans form bonds with other people and other communities and on keeping their cultures alive.*

AFTER YOU READ

EXPLORING YOUR RESPONSES

1. Although college was sometimes difficult for Laura Weber, she was motivated to do well. How important do you think motivation is to success? Explain.

2. In high school Weber hated chemistry, but she later earned two degrees in it. Why do you think people might hate certain subjects, then discover later that they like them?

3. Chemical engineers are trying to undo some of the damage our society has done to the environment. What are some of the things people do that hurt the environment?

4. The logo for Weber's company is a turtle with a picture of North America on its back. In what ways is this logo appropriate for PM Earth?

5. During the AISES meeting that Weber attended, she rediscovered her heritage. How might knowing about one's heritage help people understand themselves and their families?

UNDERSTANDING WORDS IN CONTEXT

Read the following sentences from the biography. Think about what each underlined word means. In your notebook, write what the word means as it is used in the sentence.

1. Like other Native American groups, the Mohawk see the environment and people as interdependent—they need each other for survival.

2. That light switch was chemistry—the study of what different substances are made of and what happens when they interact.

3. The logo for Laura's company is a turtle with a picture of North America on its back.

4. PM Earth is based on the idea that the best way to solve a problem is not to create one in the first place. [Laura] helps companies look for ways to <u>generate</u> less waste.

5. "I had <u>mediocre</u> grades. People were not confident that I could go to college and be successful."

RECALLING DETAILS

1. Why did Weber not learn about her Native American heritage until she was an adult?

2. Who helped Laura decide to study chemistry?

3. What is AISES?

4. What does PM Earth do?

5. What are the "three Rs" that Laura's company manages?

UNDERSTANDING INFERENCES

In your notebook, write two or three sentences from the biography that support each of the following inferences.

1. Weber had confidence in herself even when other people did not.

2. Learning about her Native American heritage greatly influenced Weber.

3. Education is important to Weber.

4. There is a need for the kind of work PM Earth does.

5. It can be difficult to start a business.

INTERPRETING WHAT YOU HAVE READ

1. How did learning about her past help Laura find her path in life?

2. How is Weber's job as environmental consultant educational to her clients?

3. What may happen at a powwow?

4. What do you think Weber would say is the key to a clean environment?

5. In what ways does Weber's job reflect her Native American heritage?

ANALYZING QUOTATIONS

Read the following quotation from the biography and answer the questions below.

> *"It was motivation. And all my life I had all these people telling me I couldn't do these things, and I wanted to prove to them that I could."*

1. What motivated Weber to succeed?

2. How do you think Weber knew she could succeed, even when other people did not? Explain.

3. Some people are motivated to try a difficult task while other people are not. How can people motivate themselves?

THINKING CRITICALLY

1. What might Veronica Cunningham have done to spark Laura's interest in chemistry?

2. Becoming an environmental engineer was not always easy for Weber. Why do you think she kept trying?

3. What do you think gives Weber the most satisfaction about her job? Why?

4. Weber's job requires knowledge of chemistry and engineering. What practical skills does a person need to succeed in business?

5. Weber states that "Indian tradition teaches us that we should all respect and love the Earth as we would our mother." In what sense is the Earth "our mother"?

FRED BEGAY

Fred Begay, Navajo physicist, studies matter and energy at the Los Alamos Scientific Laboratory in New Mexico. Begay believes that his Navajo heritage inspired his curiosity about the world and how it works.

"**H**ere at Los Alamos Scientific Laboratory, we're trying to produce and harness the same energy that makes the sun and the stars shine," says Fred Begay (buh-GAY). The Los Alamos Scientific Laboratory, which is located in New Mexico, is part of one of the largest and most advanced research institutions of its kind in the world. Thanks to Fred Begay and scientists like him, much is being learned about the mysteries of energy.

Dr. Fred Begay is a physicist, a scientist who studies matter[1] and energy. Physicists study the ways in which such things as heat, light, sound, electricity, magnetism, and atomic energy[2] affect one another. Fred defines the physicist's job in a simple way: "A scientist looks at the world as a child does, always wondering, what is it made of? What are the pieces of the pieces of the pieces?"

These are the same questions Fred began asking as a child. His Navajo heritage encouraged his curiosity about the world and how it works. "When I was a kid," he says, "I wanted to know what made it all work. I looked at the shapes of the mountains and the rocks, and I wondered how they got that way."

Fred was born in 1932 on the Ute (YOOT) Mountain Indian Reservation, in Towaoc (TOH-uh-wawk), Colorado. Fred and his family, which included four brothers and sisters, were nomads.[3] They moved from place to place, finding food where they could. They hunted, fished, and gathered roots and seeds.

1. **matter** (MAT-uhr) *n.* the basic material from which all things are made; matter takes up space and can be seen or sensed in some way
2. **atomic energy** (uh-TAHM-ihk EHN-uhr-jee) energy that is released from atoms, when they are broken apart (fission) or joined (fusion)
3. **nomads** (NOH-mads) *n. pl.* people who do not have a permanent home, but travel from place to place

They roamed the mountains of the reservations located in the Four Corners, which is the part of the United States where Utah, Colorado, New Mexico, and Arizona meet. "I was raised near and on the mountains," Fred says, "on the Navajo Reservation in Utah, the Ute Mountain Indian Reservation in Colorado, and the Southern Ute Indian Reservation in Colorado." His early years were spent learning to respect nature and to survive in it.

"My family lived a typical, traditional Navajo/Ute life with no modern utilities[4] such as electricity or running water. My parents did not speak or write English. They practiced Navajo/Ute medicine and medicine rituals. They were devoted to their work [practicing medicine]. My family and I lived in harmony with ourselves and with nature," Fred recalls. The family had few possessions, traveling with only a tent, a mattress, a few pots and pans, and other necessities. It was not an easy life, especially when it was hard to find food. Fred and his family were good hunters, but sometimes there was little game to be hunted or food to be gathered.

When Fred was almost 10 years old, his family sent him to a government boarding school for Native Americans in Ignacio, Colorado. "My parents decided I should go to school because they knew there was food there. *My* reason for going was that I thought I might find answers there to some of my questions about nature," says Fred. "I always wanted to understand natural phenomena.[5] I wanted to know what made the rainbow. I wanted to know what lightning was. I asked everyone I knew about things like that, but people either didn't think there was any sense in asking or their answers weren't exactly satisfying."

Begay's first school experience was not satisfying either. Fred was not allowed to use his Navajo name, Begay. He was given an

---

4. **utilities** (yoo–TIHL–uh–teez) *n. pl.* companies that supply homes with electricity, natural gas, water, and other services

5. **phenomena** (fuh–NAHM–uh–nuh) *n. pl.* events and experiences that can be scientifically explained

English name: Fred Willey. It was later changed to Fred Young. He never knew why it was changed. As he looks back on his experiences in the school, Fred comments, "I missed my family very much. I didn't go home for ten whole months. The people in charge didn't speak my language, and they didn't want to speak it either. We were forbidden to speak Navajo and punished if caught speaking it. Not only did they try to keep us from speaking our own language, but they also were against our going to Indian ceremonies." (See **Did You Know?** on page 149 for more information on the use of the word "Navajo.")

As the years passed, Fred stayed year-round at the school, and for a time, he lost contact with his family. Some of what he learned at the school was useful to him. However, he was never really taught to read or write in English.

At the age of 23, Fred enrolled in the University of New Mexico. The schools he had attended were not like the kind of high school that most students attend before going to college. Not only was his ability to read or write English limited, but in many ways, he was not well prepared for the challenge of college. Yet he was determined, and he was encouraged by his nation and his family.

At first Fred enrolled in engineering, but he quickly realized that physics was the field he enjoyed. It was difficult to balance his studies and work part-time to help pay the bills, but somehow Fred got by. His hardest challenge of all, though, was learning to read English at the college level.

One key learning breakthrough was unforgettable for the young physicist. As he was reading a book on the subject of light and how it works, he made a wonderful discovery. "I discovered in this book the process of how the rainbow works. As I was reading the chapter, I found myself not being able to read fast enough. I really wanted to know the total information immediately. The chapter was quite long, so I had to convince myself that I needed to be patient. For many years, my study of physics and my basic questions about natural phenomena hadn't come together. There did not seem to be any relationship between the two until this one day when I read about how the rainbow works."

In 1961, Fred graduated with a Bachelor of Science degree in physics. With financial help from the Navajo, he went on to get his master's degree two years later. Still, Fred wanted to learn more. In 1972, he earned a doctorate (Ph.D.) in physics from the University of New Mexico.

Begay's many personal and professional achievements include teaching physics at the University of New Mexico, Stanford University (in California), and the University of Maryland. He has done research and testing for several organizations including NASA (National Aeronautics and Space Administration) and a weapons laboratory. He has designed and tested satellites and the instruments that control them. Since 1972, Fred has done his research at the Los Alamos Scientific Laboratory.

Fred's journey has not been easy. In the early 1980s, Fred discarded the name Young. The name Begay is an English phonetic[6] spelling that sounds like his true Navajo family name. Bridging two cultures still can be difficult. But he feels that his Navajo upbringing, with its emphasis on the structure of nature, prepared him well for physics.

To help today's Navajo students succeed, Fred Begay has developed physics lectures in the Navajo language, which he presents to Navajo high school students. He also teaches students and elders science and math in Navajo. Begay devotes much of his time to keeping Navajo/Ute customs, language, and traditions alive, especially Navajo/Ute medicine rituals.

Begay admits he may not always understand other cultures. But he likes to work with people "who share my own attitudes towards nature, and who have a curiosity about discovering or solving many of the mysteries that make up the laws of nature." For Fred Begay, a sense of wonder and a desire to know can help to bridge the gap between peoples and cultures.

---

6. **phonetic** (foh-NEHT-ihk) *adj.* representing speech sounds

Did You Know? *In the early 1600s, Spanish explorers gave the name "Navajo" to the people they met in what is now the southwestern United States. The Navajo, however, called themselves "The Diné," which roughly means "The People." Navajos today are debating whether to officially change their name to "The Diné." Some Navajos feel that they have been known as Navajos for hundreds of years and they should keep the name. Other Navajos feel strongly that they should abolish the name that was given them and officially go by their own name.*

AFTER YOU READ

EXPLORING YOUR RESPONSES

1. Fred and his family were nomads, hunting and gathering food in the mountains. What might you like or dislike about such a life?

2. "A scientist looks at the world as a child does," Fred says. What kinds of questions did you ask about the world when you were a child?

3. At the boarding school, Fred was not allowed to speak his native language and was given a different name. How might you react if this happened to you?

4. Because he enjoyed physics, Fred was motivated to learn all that he could. What motivates you to learn?

5. Navajo teaching has traditionally been done through speaking and listening rather than through reading, writing, and other approaches. In what ways do you learn best? Explain.

UNDERSTANDING WORDS IN CONTEXT

Read the following sentences from the biography. Think about what each underlined word means. In your notebook, write what the word means as it is used in the sentence.

1. Dr. Fred Begay is a physicist, a scientist who studies matter and energy. Physicists study the ways in which such things as heat, light, sound, electricity, magnetism, and atomic energy affect one another.

2. Fred and his family . . . were nomads. They moved from place to place, finding food where they could.

3. "My family lived a typical, traditional Navajo/Ute life with no modern utilities such as electricity or running water."

4. "I always wanted to understand natural phenomena. I wanted to know what made the rainbow. I wanted to know what lightning was."

5. The name Begay is an English <u>phonetic</u> spelling that sounds like [Fred's] true Navajo family name.

RECALLING DETAILS

1. Where did Fred live when he was a child?

2. Why did Fred's parents send him to a boarding school?

3. Who was Fred Young and how did he get that name?

4. What made college difficult for Fred?

5. What has Begay designed and tested?

UNDERSTANDING INFERENCES

In your notebook, write two or three sentences from the story that support each of the following inferences.

1. Fred Begay's heritage influenced his view of nature.

2. Fred learned survival skills at a young age.

3. Fred's parents were content with their way of life.

4. Fred believes people can retain their Native American culture and still be successful in U.S. society.

5. Fred's boarding school did not value his Navajo heritage.

INTERPRETING WHAT YOU HAVE READ

1. How do you think Fred's early life influenced his choice of career?

2. Why do you think Fred feels that learning Navajo/Ute medicine helped him learn about nature?

3. Why do you think the government boarding school was run the way it was?

4. What influence do you think Fred's struggle with English has had on his work with Navajo students?

5. How does Fred feel about preserving Navajo traditions?

ANALYZING QUOATATIONS

Read the following quotation from the biography and answer the questions below.

> *"I discovered in this book the process of how the rainbow works. As I was reading . . . I found myself not being able to read fast enough. I really wanted to know the total information immediately. . . . For many years, my study of physics and my basic questions about natural phenomena hadn't come together. There did not seem to be any relationship between the two until this one day when I read about how the rainbow works."*

1. Why was Fred so excited to find out about how a rainbow is made?
2. What made Fred's discovery so important?
3. Fred had to learn both a subject and a language at the same time. What challenges have you faced? How did you overcome them?

THINKING CRITICALLY

1. Why do you think being a scientist was so important to Fred?
2. How did Fred's early life help prepare him for his career?
3. Why do you think Fred took back the name Begay after being known as Fred Young for so many years?
4. "When a Navajo student fails his or her freshman year in college, it is often because of the student's difficulty with the English language," Fred says. What difficulties do you think such a student faces?
5. Is it important for people of many cultures to enter fields like science and math? Why or why not?

LOIS STEELE

Lois Steele, Assiniboine physician, is shown here (center) with her
family. As a physician in family practice, Steele works for better
health care for Native Americans.

"I am an Indian woman physician—not a 'Medicine Woman.' Few women [in medicine] are truly Medicine Women in the traditional sense," says Lois Steele, M.D. Among the Assiniboine (uh-SIHN-uh-boyn) people, as well as other groups, being an Indian Medicine Man or Woman is a great honor and responsibility. "We must respect the wisdom and talent of the holy people and shaman[1] among us," the doctor believes. "We must respect the traditional healers and work with them to help our people."

Working to help her people has been a goal of Lois Steele's for most of her life. She was born in 1939, and grew up on the Fort Peck Reservation in Poplar, Montana. Her parents were divorced when Lois was 4 years old. As she says, "It was my mother who had the bigger influence on me. . . . There were six children, and she raised us alone. . . . [but she found time] to read to me and encouraged her children to read."

When Lois reached the 11th grade, her mother sent her to a school away from the reservation. Lois attended St. Mary's Academy for Girls in Nauvoo, Illinois. "It was a good school," Lois remembers, "but, of course, in those days [the 1950s], girls—especially Indian girls—were not supposed to like science or math. The school did not even offer advanced algebra.[2] I think they thought girls couldn't do it or wouldn't need it. Fortunately for me, one teacher, Sister Bernard, taught me some advanced algebra. I will always be grateful for that."

After high school, Lois attended Jamestown College in North Dakota. The summer of her freshman year, she married a man

---

1. **shaman** (SHAH-muhn) *n. pl.* spiritual leaders and healers

2. **algebra** (AL-juh-bruh) *n.* a type of mathematics in which symbols are used to represent numbers

from her reservation. That fall they both went to Rocky Mountain College in Montana. At Rocky Mountain, Lois's leadership potential[3] began to surface. She became president of the junior class and was elected dormitory president. She did well, especially excelling in science.

When Lois's husband joined the army and was stationed at Fort Carson, Colorado, Lois transferred to Colorado College in Colorado Springs. There she earned a Bachelor of Arts degree in 1961.

For several years following graduation, Lois taught at various junior high and high schools in small Montana towns. She taught everything: math and science, physical education, English, advanced algebra, and more. If there was a need, she filled it. She coached basketball, track and field, and gymnastics. She tried to give her students a love of learning.

While she was teaching, Steele attended graduate school in the summers. She was awarded a National Science Foundation Fellowship to attend the University of Montana in Missoula. She got her master's degree in biology there in 1969, graduating with top grades.

In 1968, after 10 years of marriage, Lois and her husband divorced. From this point on, Lois raised her two daughters by herself. In spite of these challenges, Lois took a step that was to change her life. She decided to go to medical school.

A VISTA (Volunteers in Service to America) worker on the reservation told Lois how to go about taking the Medical College Admissions Test. Lois took the test and did well. But she did not know how to apply to medical school, and few people could give her advice. One local doctor did take an interest and told her how to apply to Wayne State Medical School in Michigan. Lois obtained an interview[4] at Wayne State. She used her own money to travel to Detroit to discuss her application.

---

3. **potential** (poh-TEHN-shuhl) *n.* hidden talent

4. **interview** (IHN-tuhr-vyoo) *n.* a formal meeting held to determine a person's qualifications for a position

In the interview, Steele was told she was "a poor risk, because American Indians didn't do well in medical school." The interviewer also told her that some admissions committee members felt women should be home with their children. He himself thought that women did not practice medicine as often as men after receiving their medical degrees. For this reason, women were not "good investments." The interviewer felt Lois was a good candidate[5] for the school. However, he doubted he could convince the admissions committee of this. Lois asked the interviewer why he had asked her to travel to Detroit for the interview when it was obvious the committee had already rejected her. He answered, "The committee was curious. They don't have many applicants like you." Their curiosity had cost Lois hard-earned money.

That was not the first time Lois had experienced discrimination. It was disheartening,[6] but she did not give up. From 1970-1973 she taught, coached women's basketball and track, and counseled women students at Dawson College in Glendive, Montana.

Lois's fellow teachers at Dawson respected her, electing her president of the faculty in 1972. Lois learned how to negotiate and bargain for higher pay for the teachers. She also learned to write proposals to win grants[7] to pay for special programs and services. For example, she won a grant for a program designed to meet the special needs of minority students on her campus.

By 1973, things were beginning to change. Some colleges were beginning to seek out women and other minority students. Said Lois, "Just four years after my first rejection from medical school, I found I had ten schools interested in me!"

---

5. **candidate** (KAN-duh-dayt) *n.* someone who is qualified for the position he or she seeks

6. **disheartening** (dihs-HAHRT-uhn-ihng) *adj.* causing to lose courage

7. **grants** (GRANTS) *n. pl.* money from the government and other organizations for special programs or projects

Lois was struck by a glaring need in the world of medical schools, procedures, and requirements. She felt that there was no one to lend a hand to Native Americans who wanted to pursue a health career, so Lois decided to help Native Americans enter the health field. She served as the first director of a new program called Indians into Medicine, or INMED. The program was started in the spring of 1973 by representatives from 22 reservations in North Dakota, South Dakota, Nebraska, Montana, and Wyoming. (See **Did You Know?** on page 158 for more information on INMED.)

As Director of INMED, Lois Steele worked with her small staff to support Native Americans interested in a medical profession. They worked with the financial aid[8] offices of schools and counseled would-be health professionals. They also helped students believe in themselves. "I remembered the first time I applied to a medical school. I did not know how the game was played," Lois recalls. Now she wanted others to know how to play the game–and win.

In the fall of 1974, Lois started medical school at the University of Minnesota in Duluth. It was difficult, and at times she was tempted to give up. Yet Steele excelled. She was named the Outstanding Woman Medical Student of her school in 1976. She received her medical degree in 1977. Steele then completed the on-the-job training required to become a licensed physician, certified in Family Practice.

Lois Steele has practiced family medicine on several reservations. She has a special interest in substance abuse and women's health issues. Currently, Lois is a medical researcher stationed with the Indian Health Service (IHS) in Arizona. She serves on the IHS National Institutional Review Board. She is also a physician in an IHS women's health clinic and a lecturer at the University of Arizona. In addition, Steele remains interested in INMED. She helps the organization however she can.

---

8. **financial aid** (feye-NAN-shuhl AYD) money awarded to needy students so they can pursue college educations

The list of honors and awards that Lois Steele has achieved is a long one. Along the way, she has never forgotten her roots. She strives for better health care for Native Americans. Her own recent research has focused, for example, on these topics: AIDS education for Native Americans, home health care for Native American cancer patients, and leading causes of death among certain Native American groups. In doing her research and offering her services as a doctor, Steele respects the traditions of Native Americans. She looks for ways that her modern training and knowledge can work effectively within those traditions. Have the work and the sacrifice been worth it?

As she looks back, Lois comments on the stress she had in medical school. "In my first year, I felt so isolated. At first I thought it was because I was Indian." The competitive atmosphere was uncomfortable for many Native Americans because in their cultures, competitiveness is not an admired characteristic. Yet, Lois found that most students experience the same isolation in their first year. She is happy to report that her class learned to work together and support each other.

"Preparing for a health career requires dedication and hard work," Lois says, "but achieving any worthwhile goal in life usually does. I am thankful for the opportunity to practice medicine. I am also thankful for all the people who kept me going when I was discouraged. . . . Yes," says the doctor, "it has been worth it."

> ***Did You Know?*** *INMED sponsors a Summer Institute each year. For several weeks, Native American junior high and high school students planning to enter health careers go to the University of North Dakota campus. There they take math and science enrichment courses, discuss their cultural heritage, and enjoy outdoor activities such as hiking, canoeing, and swimming. Similar programs are designed by INMED to help college-level students to strengthen their math, science, communication, writing, computer, and test-taking skills.*

AFTER YOU READ

EXPLORING YOUR RESPONSES

1. Lois was grateful for the teacher who agreed to teach her advanced algebra. What subjects would you like to learn?

2. Lois not only taught math and science, but she also coached both girls' and boys' athletic teams. How important do you think sports is in school?

3. Some people did not encourage Lois to go to medical school. How might you advise someone who was discouraged in this way?

4. As the first director of INMED, Steele had to figure out how to do a brand new job. When you tackle something new, what skills do you use?

5. Lois was elected faculty president at Dawson College. What do you think makes a person a good leader?

UNDERSTANDING WORDS IN CONTEXT

Read the following sentences from the biography. Think about what each underlined word means. In your notebook, write what the word means as it is used in the sentence.

1. "We must respect the wisdom and talent of the holy people and shaman among us," the doctor believes. "We must respect the traditional healers and work with them to help our people."

2. Lois's leadership potential began to surface. She became president of the junior class.

3. Lois obtained an interview at Wayne State. She used her own money to travel to Detroit to discuss her application.

4. The interviewer felt Lois was a good candidate for the school. However, he doubted he could convince the admissions committee of this.

5. She learned to write proposals to win <u>grants</u> to pay for special programs and services.

RECALLING DETAILS

1. Which courses were not available at St. Mary's Academy?

2. What happened at Lois's first interview when she was applying to medical school?

3. What did Steele learn to do while president of the faculty at Dawson College?

4. Why was INMED founded?

5. Why did Lois feel isolated in medical school?

UNDERSTANDING INFERENCES

In your notebook, write two or three sentences from the biography that support each of the following inferences.

1. As recently as the 1970s, there were few Native Americans entering the health care field.

2. Lois had to overcome discrimination as a student.

3. Lois's heritage influenced the way she felt about medicine.

4. Cultural differences can make medical school particularly challenging.

5. Lois Steele has given of herself to her people.

INTERPRETING WHAT YOU HAVE READ

1. Lois's mother chose to send her to high school away from the reservation. What does this tell you about her mother's view of the reservation's schools?

2. How do you think her mother's attitude towards reading influenced Lois's life?

3. How does Steele feel about the work and the importance of Medicine Men and Women?

4. How did being a Native American and a woman affect Lois's dream of becoming a doctor?

5. Why do you think Lois chose to teach on the reservation and later, to practice medicine there?

ANALYZING QUOTATIONS

Read the following quotation from the biography and answer the questions below.

"I remembered the first time I applied to a medical school. I did not know how the game was played."

1. Why do you think Lois refers to applying to medical school as a "game"?

2. What do you think Lois learned from her experience in applying to medical school?

3. Have you ever felt that you did not "know the rules" for something you wanted to accomplish? How did you solve the problem?

THINKING CRITICALLY

1. Why do you think Lois chose to go into medicine?

2. Think about the path Lois took to get through medical school. How did her cultural heritage affect her journey?

3. Lois said that fierce competition often isolated medical students from each other. In what ways can competition can be a bad thing? In what ways can it be a good thing?

4. Why do Steele and others believe it is important to have Native Americans in the medical profession?

5. How did Lois's position as head of the faculty at Dawson College prepare her for her role as director of INMED?

CULTURAL CONNECTIONS

THINKING ABOUT WHAT PEOPLE DO

1. Imagine you are trying to choose between the careers described in this unit. Choose one, then write a short paragraph telling why you might enjoy the work. Give examples to support your ideas.

2. Imagine that you could interview one of the people in this unit. Make a list of five questions you would ask the person. Then explain why you chose these questions.

3. With a partner, choose one of the people in this unit. Write a short skit in which you act out a scene from that person's life. Use dialogue that helps tell the story. Present your skit to the class.

THINKING ABOUT CULTURE

1. Describe how two of the people in this unit experienced discrimination in their lives. Tell how their experiences were similar and how they were different.

2. The environment is important to many of the people of this unit. How did the cultural backgrounds of two of them influence the way they view the land and its resources?

3. Name two organizations mentioned in this unit that encourage Native Americans to choose careers in the sciences and math. How can such organizations help young people?

4. Choose two people in this unit and explain how their cultures influenced their choice of career.

5. What did you discover in this unit about overcoming barriers and problems? Do you think a person's cultural background can help both to create and to solve such problems? Give examples from the biographies to support your opinions.

BUILDING RESEARCH SKILLS

Work with a partner to complete the following activity.

The people discussed in this unit come from different parts of the United States. Choose one location for further study, and make a list of the things you might like to learn about that place. You might ask the following questions:

Hint: The Bibliography at the back of this book will give you a list of books and articles that can help you begin your research.

☆ How has the population of the area changed since the 1400s?

☆ How did the land look in the 1400s?

☆ How does it look now?

☆ How has the government changed since the 1400s?

Hint: Use a historical atlas and other reference materials to investigate the area you have chosen.

Next, go to the library to find the answers to your questions.

Prepare a picture time line, including five or six important facts about the area. Draw or copy a picture and write a short description that explains each fact. Remember to present your facts chronologically, or in time order, on your time line. Use facts that tell about the people, the geography, the environment, the history, and the culture. Display your time line on your class bulletin board.

Hint: As you research your chosen location, write each fact on a separate index card. Write the date to which the fact refers at the top of the card. Then organize your index cards chronologically.

Extending Your Studies

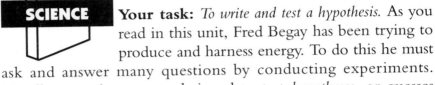

Your task: *To write and test a hypothesis.* As you read in this unit, Fred Begay has been trying to produce and harness energy. To do this he must ask and answer many questions by conducting experiments. Usually, experiments are designed to test *hypotheses*, or guesses that scientists like Begay make that are based on facts.

When a scientist tests a hypothesis, he or she uses the following procedure:

☆ *The question:* Can geraniums survive without water?

☆ *Available information:* Geraniums do not grow in deserts, and other plants tend to die if they are not watered.

☆ *The hypothesis:* A geranium cannot survive without water.

☆ *The experiment:* Take two geraniums and place them side by side on a windowsill so that they receive equal amounts of light. Water one geranium every three or four days, but do not water the other geranium at all. At the end of one month, compare the two geraniums.

☆ *Findings:* The geranium that has been watered has many new, bright green leaves. The geranium that has not been watered has lost most of its leaves and is brown and withered. The hypothesis is confirmed: Geraniums cannot survive without water.

Follow the scientific process described above to write and test your own hypothesis. You may wish to consult your science textbook or your science teacher for ideas of hypotheses to test. Share the results of your experiment with your class.

VISUAL ARTS **Your task:** *To design a logo for a company concerned with environmental protection.* The logo designed for Laura Weber's company, PM Earth, consists of a turtle with a picture of North America on its back. This logo is especially appealing because it symbolizes Weber's heritage as well as her concerns for the environment.

Imagine that you own a consulting company that helps businesses protect the environment. Write a paragraph that describes what your company does, then design a logo that shows your company's concern for the environment. Remember that the best logos are simple in design and use symbols rather than words.

HEALTH **Your task:** *To compose a list of safety rules for bicycling, skating, and skateboarding.* Doctors, like Lois Steele, are pleased when their patients focus on health promotion. When this occurs, they see fewer people who are suffering from preventable problems.

You can help protect yourself and your friends from injury by reminding one another of safety rules. Work with several other students to create a list of rules that should be followed when you are "on wheels." Choose one of these methods of transportation:

☆ skateboarding

☆ in-line skating

☆ rollerskating

☆ bicycling

Make a list of safety equipment that should be worn, rules that should be followed, and activities that carry unacceptable risks. Then create a class poster for your school to remind all students how to ride on wheels—safely.

WRITING WORKSHOP

In Unit 2, you wrote a biographical sketch about a friend. For this unit, write a **biographical sketch of someone in your family or community**. You might choose a family member who is particularly special to you, or a teacher you know and admire. Your purpose in writing this biography is to show your friends and classmates why this person is memorable or noteworthy.

PREWRITING

In this *prewriting* step, you will gather information by conducting an interview. Here are suggestions for getting started.

Select a subject: First, you must choose a subject. Think about the people in your family—not just those living with you but other relatives as well. Someone in your community is also a possibility—perhaps someone who has done or achieved something special. In your notebook, jot down three or four names and some information about each person. Next, select the person who most interests you, who you think will interest others, and about whom you can gather information.

List questions: Think about what you already know about the person by listing some of your impressions. You might note the person's age, occupation, place of birth, or relationship to you. Jot down facts you can observe as well. Details like these will help you draw a clear picture of your subject. As you explore what you know, you will begin to see what you *do not* know. Start listing questions you have about the person.

☆ What was your childhood like?

☆ What kind of work do you do?

☆ What kind of schooling did you have?

☆ Who are your heroes?

☆ What are some of your goals and achievements?

Organize your questions into different categories. That will help you later when you write about the person. Prepare more questions than you think you might need, just in case the interview proceeds more quickly than you had planned.

Do some research about the person: If the person grew up in Oklahoma, for example, you might research that area of the country. Find out about the person's heritage. Read about his or her cultural background, if appropriate. You might need to add more questions to your list.

Arrange for the interview: Set a time and a place that are convenient for both of you. Allow at least an hour of quiet, uninterrupted time.

Conduct the interview: Be polite. Above all, be a good listener. Start with a question that cannot be answered with "yes" or "no." You might begin, for example, with "Tell me about. . . ." Be flexible and ready to explore areas you had not expected. Take careful notes. If you want to record the interview, be sure to ask the subject's permission. Thank your subject when the interview is over.

Organize your notes. While the interview is still fresh in your mind, go over your notes and begin to organize them. Add details if you can. Then decide what your focus will be. You cannot include every detail about the person. Concentrate on your purpose: What is it that makes this person memorable? What do you want your readers to learn about the person? You may want to use *chronological order,* or time order, to organize your notes.

DRAFTING

Once you have organized your notes and determined your focus, you can begin *drafting* your biography. First, decide on an interesting way to start your biography. You could begin with a quotation, either from the subject or from someone else. You could begin by telling a story about the person. Whichever way you choose, catch your reader's interest right away.

As you write your draft, do not worry about making it perfect. Get your ideas down in a clear, understandable way. You will check for word usage and spelling errors later.

REVISING

Put your biographical sketch aside for a day or two. Then, with the help of another student who will act as your editor, evaluate and *revise* your work. See the directions for writers and student editors below.

Directions for Writers: Read your work aloud, listening to how it flows. Then ask yourself these questions:

☆ Does my opening hold the reader's attention?

☆ Am I *showing,* not *telling,* what happened?

☆ Did I include interesting details?

☆ Does my description make my subject come alive?

Make notes for your next draft or revise your work before you give it to a student editor. Then, ask the student editor to read your work. Listen carefully to his or her suggestions. If they seem helpful, use them to improve your writing when you revise your work.

Directions for Student Editors: Read the work carefully and respectfully, remembering that your purpose is to help the writer do his or her best work. Keep in mind that an editor should always make positive, helpful comments that point to specific parts of the essay. After you read the work, use the following questions to help you direct your comments:

☆ What did I like most about the biographical sketch?

☆ What would I like to know more about?

☆ Can I see the scene or event in my mind?

☆ Do I feel that I know the subject?

PROOFREADING

When you are satisfied that your writing says what you want it to say, check it carefully for errors in spelling, punctuation, capitalization, grammar, and usage. Then make a neat, final copy of your biography.

PUBLISHING

After you have revised your writing, you are ready to publish it. Design a cover for your biography. Create an image that helps catch the reader's eye, but that also says something about the subject of the biography. Then read your biographical sketch to the class in a People of Note presentation.

NATIVE AMERICANS IN EDUCATION AND PUBLIC SERVICE

In this unit, you will read about six Native Americans who have some similar talents and goals. They also share a commitment to helping people preserve their individual rights and heritages. Read to discover what they have in common as well as what sets them apart.

Curator **Rick Hill** feels that art can help keep Native American cultures (like his own Tuscarora culture) alive. "Through the arts, people will get to see what Indians are saying and thinking," he says.

In the House of Representatives and then in the Senate, **Ben Nighthorse Campbell** has served many causes, including human rights. Campbell explains, "I vote independently. . . . I wasn't elected to become one of the Washington crowd. It's just not me."

Anthropologist **Shirley Hill Witt**, of Akwesasne (ah-kwuh-SAHS-nee) Mohawk heritage says, "The path of my life has . . . left me with an undeniable need to participate in matters concerning civil–human–rights."

Chairperson of the Tohono O'Odham (toh-HOH-noh OH AHD-uhm), **Tom Segundo** fought to preserve the rights of his people. "The only way anyone can come on the reservation and establish a business," he said, "is by permission of the tribe. It's a privilege."

Laura Waterman Wittstock, a Seneca, has worked for the equal rights of Native American journalists. She says, "A free press and an adequate press are important for the future of the Indian people."

Nisqually (nihs-KWAH-lee) environmentalist **Billy Frank** says, "We don't have to take the last tree or the last drop of water. . . . We have to give a little, all of us."

Consider as you read these biographies how each person's personality and career have allowed him or her to serve others.

RICK HILL

Rick Hill, Tuscarora museum curator, believes that art is a way of preserving tradition. At the National Museum of the American Indian in Washington, D.C., Hill is organizing an exhibit about Native American cultures.

Children dream about becoming dancers, astronauts, or firefighters when they grow up. Few, if any, dream about becoming a curator[1] of art. But if children knew how exciting and important the job of curator is, they might add it to their list. Curators study art and collect it for museums. They help educate people about various cultures and periods of time. For Rick Hill, being a curator is a way of keeping the culture of his nation and of other Native American groups alive. "Through the arts, people will get to see what Indians are saying and thinking," he says.

Richard Hill was born in 1951 in New York. He is a member of the Tuscarora (tuhs-kuh-RAW-ruh) Nation of the Iroquois (IHR-uh-kwoi) league and has lived on a reservation most of his life. (See **Did You Know?** on page 177 for more information about the Tuscarora Nation.) Rick believes that art helps keep culture alive. "My grandfather was a woodworker and my grandmother was a quiltmaker," Rick once told an interviewer. "My uncle was a stone carver. Art was a [way] to keep us all together . . . and also to supplement[2] income."

Many members of Rick's family were ironworkers, working in mills to produce heavy iron or steel products. Most people in his family and community assumed[3] that he would be an ironworker, too. But in his teens, he decided he could express himself and explore his heritage through art. "It [art] was a way to talk and share things, a way of recalling tradition. Among the Iroquois, the sort of group thinking we do is helped by the fact

1. **curator** (KYOO-rayt-uhr) *n.* a person who decides what will be displayed in a collection or exhibit, especially for a museum or library
2. **supplement** (SUHP-luh-muhnt) *v.* to add to
3. **assumed** (uh-SOOMD) *v.* to suppose or take for granted

that we have such a rich oral history.[4] The artist keeps bringing that out."

It is difficult, however, to make a living as an artist. Did he have the talent? "When I turned eighteen, I had to make a decision," Hill explains. "Do I want to work with my dad or do I want to go to art school?"

Hill was torn between wanting to please his family and wanting to study art and photography. He was afraid to tell his dad he wanted to be a photographer, not an ironworker. When they talked about Rick's desire, however, his father was supportive. His advice was that Rick should be the best photographer he could be. Rick enrolled in the Art Institute of Chicago.

At the Art Institute, Rick studied and worked with some of the most prominent[5] photographers of the time. At first, he remembers, "I thought I wouldn't photograph Indians. I thought that would be too easy . . . that art was something else, something bigger than life."

Hill would soon learn that what seemed "small" and familiar to him was "bigger than life," after all. A non–Native American friend was photographing Native Americans, but felt he was not successful. He said to Rick, "Indians are the toughest people to photograph." Hill told his friend that a photographer could not just walk in and take good pictures of people he or she did not understand. The people had to *matter* to the photographer. Rick's friend replied simply, "Then *you* have to do it. Photograph Indian people."

Rick Hill realized the truth of his own words. The closer a photographer feels to the subject, the better the picture will be. He then began to photograph Native Americans–in Chicago, at home, everywhere he could. "When I realized that art had this

---

4. **oral history** historical information that is gathered and preserved in spoken form, often passed down from one generation to the next

5. **prominent** (PRAHM-uh-nuhnt) *adj.* widely and favorably known

ability to communicate a sense of communal identity, as well as my feelings of individuality, then that's the direction [my art] took."

Hill was also painting at the same time, but there was a problem. He had trouble exhibiting[6] his paintings and photographs. If he could not exhibit his work, how could he sell it? Hill found that some art gallery owners and museum directors took Native American art seriously only if it was traditional, like a piece of pottery or a blanket. "Stereotypes about Indians make it difficult [for people] to see the Indian with his feathers removed," Rick concluded.

Hill knew that things had to change if Native American art were to flourish. "My frustration at not being able to sell my photographs or exhibit them led me to [my present work]," he explains. The first step was educating people about the richness and variety of Native American culture.

In 1977, Rick Hill joined the faculty of the State University of New York (SUNY) in Buffalo. There he taught art and Native American literature and promoted Native American art among gallery owners and art-world leaders. He became known for his ability to put together exciting shows. Organizing an exhibit takes a great deal of work and knowledge. It also requires "people skills," the ability to communicate clearly and to get the best out of each artist. Rick Hill was proving that he had this blend of talents.

The word got out. In 1990, The Institute of American Indian Arts (IAIA) in Santa Fe, New Mexico, offered Hill a job. The IAIA needed a director for its new museum of Native American art. This was an important, challenging opportunity. Hill accepted the job and moved with his family to Santa Fe.

Hill supervised the renovation of a large, old building as it was turned into a state-of-the-art exhibition and storage space. He

---

6. **exhibiting** (ehg-ZIHB-iht-ihng) *v.* presenting or showing, usually in a museum or gallery

hired a staff and got busy planning temporary exhibits. He also worked on the museum's permanent collection, called "Creativity Is Our Tradition." Hill saw it as a right and a responsibility to "interpret Indian art through Indian eyes."

In June of 1992, Rick Hill moved from his post in Santa Fe to become Assistant Director for Public Programs at the new National Museum of the American Indian (NMAI), at the Smithsonian Institution. In 1846, the U.S. Congress had set up the collection of museums called the Smithsonian to give a full picture of the nation's cultural achievements. Oddly, though, a museum that specializes in Native American culture and art did not exist until 1992. In that year, legislation was passed under the leadership of several people, including Senator Ben Nighthorse Campbell (see his biography on page 181), that established NMAI.

Although the building that will be the NMAI's permanent home in Washington, D.C., will not be ready until about 1999, the museum is already "open for business." It is currently located in the Custom House in New York City.

One of Hill's first challenges at the Smithsonian was to curate an exhibit called "Pathways of Tradition," a collection of more than 100 items. These items represented Native American artistry spanning hundreds of years. Rick consulted with 28 Native American artists, religious leaders, educators, and museum directors to help give the public a "wide-angle" view on Native American creativity.

Rick and others involved in the new museum were not only interested in *what* was displayed, however. They were also concerned about *how* the art was displayed. Hill commented, "Indian art is often presented as primitive. While other works in the Smithsonian were placed on pedestals and well-lit . . . the Indian art was jumbled together in a single display case. Equally shocking was how few pieces were shown." He also noted that most contemporary[7] Native American art was displayed at the

---

7. **contemporary** (kuhn-TEHM-puh-rair-ee) *adj.* of the present time; modern

Smithsonian's Museum of Natural History instead of at the National Gallery, where modern art is usually shown.

According to museum director Richard West, Jr., a Cheyenne, what is needed is "an institution of living culture"—a place where people can connect with the life, literature, language, history, and art of all native people of the Western Hemisphere. In Hill's words, "What I'm hoping is that the museum will be like a conversation with Indians."

Rick Hill continues to live on the reservation, commuting from New York to his job in Washington, D.C. "A lot of people think success is getting ahead, leaving the Indian behind. But we have to take care of our own because there's no one else to do it. What I'm looking at now . . . is how am I going to remain Indian, make a living, change people's thinking about Indians, and remain true to some sort of internal, core belief? It's a constant struggle in my life." Rick Hill's struggle is a gift to the country. He is helping to keep the legacy[8] of Native American people alive.

> **Did You Know?** *The Tuscarora belong to a league, or association, of Native American groups called the Six Nations. The groups spoke the same language and lived in northern New York State when the league was founded, about 1720. During the 1700s and 1800s, the Iroquois used beads called wampum (WAHM-puhm) in their artwork. They decorated their buckskin clothing and moccasins with beads, as well as with porcupine quills, moose hair, thistle, bird feathers, and other natural materials. Most of the beadwork designs reflect the flowers, leaves, and trees of the Iroquois. Wampum was also used as money and in religious ceremonies.*

8. **legacy** (LEHG-uh-see) *n.* something handed down from an ancestor

AFTER YOU READ

EXPLORING YOUR RESPONSES

1. Rick Hill's grandfather was a woodworker, his grandmother a quiltmaker, and his uncle a stone carver. If you could be any kind of artist, what kind would you choose? Explain.

2. Hill believes that people should learn about and preserve their heritage. How would you advise someone to learn more about his or her heritage?

3. Rick's friend encouraged him to photograph Native Americans, which helped Rick find his path in life. Describe a time when encouragement you have given or received has been helpful.

4. Hill has dedicated himself to making Native American art available to people. What do you think art can teach people?

5. Hill has often chosen to show people rather than to tell about them. Do you prefer words or pictures as ways of sharing your ideas? Explain.

UNDERSTANDING WORDS IN CONTEXT

Read the following sentences from the biography. Think about what each underlined word means. In your notebook, write what the word means as it is used in the sentence.

1. But if children knew how exciting and important the job of curator is, they might add it to their list. Curators study art and collect it for museums.

2. "Art was a [way] to keep us all together . . . and also to supplement income."

3. At the Art Institute, Rick studied and worked with some of the most prominent photographers of the time.

4. [Rick] had trouble exhibiting his paintings and photographs. If he could not exhibit his work, how could he sell it?

5. He also noted that most <u>contemporary</u> Native American art was displayed at the Smithsonian's Museum of Natural History instead of at the National Gallery, where modern art is usually shown.

RECALLING DETAILS

1. What decision did Rick Hill make when he was 18 years old?

2. In what kind of art was Hill first interested?

3. Why did Hill decide to become a curator?

4. Why has Hill lived on a reservation most of his life?

5. Describe the job of a museum curator.

UNDERSTANDING INFERENCES

In your notebook, write two or three sentences from the biography that support each of the following inferences.

1. Art can be a form of communication.

2. Photographers should understand their subjects.

3. Rick Hill is not afraid of changing directions in his life.

4. There are many careers open to someone interested in art.

5. Rick believes in exploring one's heritage.

INTERPRETING WHAT YOU HAVE READ

1. How might Hill's photography and work as a curator help to preserve Native American history?

2. Why did Rick think that photographing Native Americans would be "too easy"?

3. How did stereotypes about Native Americans get in the way of artists' exhibiting their work?

4. Why do you suppose Rick sees interpreting "Indian art through Indian eyes" as both a right and a responsibility?

5. Why is it important that Congress has approved a National Museum of the American Indian?

ANALYZING QUOTATIONS

Read the following quotation from the biography and answer the questions below.

> *"A lot of people think success is getting ahead, leaving the Indian behind. But we have to take care of our own because there's no one else to do it."*

1. Explain what you think Rick Hill means when he says "we have to take care of our own."

2. In what ways might a Native American "leave the Indian behind" as he or she becomes successful?

3. In what ways might a person take care of his or her own?

THINKING CRITICALLY

1. Why do you think Hill chose such a different path from that of his father?

2. Why do you think that Native American art was displayed in the Museum of Natural History?

3. Hill was concerned about stereotypes of Native Americans. What stereotypes do you think concerned him and why?

4. Why do you suppose there has never been a national museum for Native American art?

5. If you could create an "institute of living culture" what would you include in your exhibit?

BEN NIGHTHORSE CAMPBELL

Ben Nighthorse Campbell, Northern Cheyenne senator, waves to a crowd of supporters. As a senator, Nighthorse Campbell votes independently and fights for causes he believes in.

In 1986, a newly elected congressman entered the floor of the U.S. House of Representatives in Washington, D.C. His colleagues[1] raised their eyebrows at his string tie and leather jacket. The House of Representatives has a dress code that requires male members to wear suits and neckties. But the new congressman from Colorado, Ben Nighthorse Campbell, had gotten permission to forgo the tie required by the code. Instead he would dress the way he had for many years. In 1992, Nighthorse Campbell left the House after he was elected to represent Colorado in the U.S. Senate. At that time, his appearance was no longer making news; he was. Ben Nighthorse Campbell is the first Native American to serve in the Senate since 1929.

Campbell was born in 1933 in the small town of Auburn, California. His father was a member of the Cheyenne nation. His mother was an immigrant from Portugal. Ben's childhood was a difficult one. His father was an alcoholic who rarely worked and often disappeared mysteriously for months. When Ben was 5 years old, he and his sister Alberta were put in a children's home because his mother could not care for them by herself. Ben's mother had tuberculosis, a very serious disease that often affects the lungs.

In the 1950s, the family's financial situation began to improve. Ben's mother was building a successful grocery business in their hometown. However, having some money was little consolation.[2] His mother's illness and his father's frequent absences made Ben both strong and insecure. In this background

1. **colleagues** (KAHL-eegz) *n. pl.* fellow workers

2. **consolation** (kahn-suh-LAY-shuhn) *n.* comfort; something that eases sadness

lay the clues to his later rebelliousness,[3] creativity, and determination.

When Ben dropped out of high school in 1950, he was not failing his classes at Placer High School in northern California. Many of his teachers liked him, though he sometimes lacked self-discipline and wound up in detention after school. He even liked some of his classes—art, shop, and physical education were his favorites. So why did Ben drop out six months before graduation? To some people, Ben's decision to leave high school was quite understandable. He just had to get away.

Ben wanted freedom. He wanted to see the world, so he joined the Air Force. The Air Force sent him to Korea, where he lived for one year. While there, Ben earned a high school equivalency degree, which meant he could go on with his education, but he would not receive a high school diploma. When he returned to the United States, he used the equivalency degree to enroll at San Jose State University. While working toward his bachelor's degree, which he earned in 1957, Campbell also studied judo,[4] a Japanese martial[5] art. What he liked about judo was that it required both physical and mental skill—and he was good at it.

Judo trains people in self-defense. It is also a philosophy, or way of thinking. Judo teaches students that defeat and loss are not "bad." They are the stepping-stones to strength. This was an important lesson for Ben. His judo coach taught him not to look at everything in life as a win or lose, good or bad situation. He learned that losses contain valuable lessons and that defeats can actually be victories.

Campbell became a judo expert. In 1960, he moved to Japan to train for the 1964 Olympic games in Tokyo. In 1963, he won the gold medal in the Pan-American Games. However, in the 1964

3. **rebelliousness** (rih-BEHL-yuhs-nuhs) *n.* active resistance to authority; defiance

4. **judo** (JOO-doh) *n.* a Japanese sport, and a means of self-defense that does not use weapons

5. **martial** (MAHR-shuhl) *adj.* showing readiness to fight; warlike

Olympics, Campbell did not do as well. Because of trouble with his knee, he finished fourth. By now he knew that losing was not the same as failing. Judo had given Campbell a belief in his own abilities—including the ability to rally[6] after a loss or disappointment.

When Campbell returned to the United States, he turned that confidence into a successful jewelry-making business. From the age of 12, Ben had turned scraps of metal and colored stones into jewelry. It was a craft he had learned from his father, who had learned jewelry making from Navajo artists. Over the years, Campbell became one of the most well-known jewelry makers in the United States. In 1977, Ben, his wife, and two children moved to southern Colorado. They lived on a ranch on the Ute Reservation, where he made jewelry and raised horses until 1982.

Making jewelry awakened in Ben the desire to explore his Native American heritage. When he was a boy, Ben's father had taught him *not* to tell people he was Native American. In fact, Ben's father often told people that he was part Scot and part Spanish, instead of Cheyenne. According to Ben's father, being Native American meant facing prejudice and feeling isolated. Campbell decided to accept that challenge. He would no longer hide his Native American identity.

Ben learned stories about his great-grandfather, who had fought with the legendary warrior Crazy Horse. (See **Did You Know?** on page 186 for more information about Crazy Horse.) Ben also began to dress in cowboy hats and string ties. He explains, "I don't get haircuts. Did it a few times, didn't like it. I started letting my hair grow in 1965. I was into ponytails long before [they were a trend]." In 1980, at a ceremony on the Northern Cheyenne reservation in Montana, Ben changed his name from Campbell to Nighthorse Campbell.

In 1982, Ben's life took another sharp turn. One evening, he dropped into a meeting of the local Democratic party to look for a college classmate. Until then, Nighthorse Campbell had not paid much attention to politics. The party leaders were discussing

---

6. rally (RAL-ee) *v.* to bring back into action

a problem. No one wanted to run against the popular opponent. They felt that Ben might be just the person to try. He was an "outsider" to politics and the party leaders thought the voters might like a new face. To everyone's surprise, Nighthorse Campbell not only won the Democratic nomination for a seat in the Colorado state legislature. He also won the election, and served in the Colorado legislature until 1986. At that time, Ben Nighthorse Campbell was elected to the U.S. House of Representatives. The high school dropout had achieved an honor and taken on a responsibility few people ever do.

Nighthorse Campbell acted in Washington as he had in Colorado. "I don't follow the party line," he explains. "I'm even in trouble sometimes with the [Democratic] leadership. I vote independently, because that's the way I want to do it. . . . I've never believed in the melting pot theory that you put a bunch of people together and all of a sudden they look alike and act alike. I wasn't elected to become one of the Washington crowd. It's just not me."

While in the House, Nighthorse Campbell fought for causes he believed in, including Native American rights. For instance, he got the name of the Custer Battlefield National Monument changed to Little Bighorn National Battlefield. This monument in Montana commemorates[7] a battle in which Native Americans defeated U.S. soldiers led by General George Armstrong Custer. Nighthorse Campbell believed that the monument should be dedicated to the Native Americans who died there in 1876–not to the General who attacked them. He explains, "This is the only battlefield I've ever heard of being named after a loser."

Successful as he had become, one thing continued to bother Ben Nighthorse Campbell. He had never received a "real" high school diploma. In 1991, Ben called the principal at Placer High School and asked if he might finally get the piece of paper he had earned through many years studying issues of concern to U.S. citizens. The school's 300 seniors voted to let Ben come

---

7. **commemorates** (kuh-MEHM-uh-rayts) *v.* honors; keeps the memory of something alive

back for his diploma. Some people wondered why a national leader would bother about a high school diploma, especially when he had an equivalency degree. He explains, "I wanted to make that statement that I finally finished. The actual diploma is important to me. I get called on a lot to speak to Indian youngsters. It just seemed to me if I was going to tell them to get their diploma, I needed to have mine."

Teenage rebel, judo expert, jewelry maker, representative, senator—Ben Nighthorse Campbell has had many roles. Which suits him best? "I really think if I had to choose between politics and art, I'd stay with the art world," said Ben after his Senate victory in 1992. "It's a lifestyle of almost total freedom. . . . Now it's my hobby, my escape mode. It's a form of therapy to take my mind off the political thing. You were born with a certain kind of soul in you. It's something I don't think you should imprison or hold back. Art, in the Indian way of believing, is a gift you're born with."

> **Did You Know?** The Northern Cheyenne, the nation to which Ben Nighthorse Campbell belongs, fought in the Battle of the Little Bighorn against General Custer and the U.S. army. The battle was part of a "land war" over the Black Hills of what is now South Dakota. This land had been "given" to Native Americans by treaty with the U.S. government, but when gold was discovered there, the U.S. government tried to buy the land or the right to mine the gold. The Native Americans refused because this land was sacred to them. General Custer and his 225 U.S. soldiers were killed at Little Bighorn, but even though the Native Americans were victorious, their victory did not save their land or protect their way of life. Eventually, the U.S. government forced them out of the Black Hills and onto reservations. Crazy Horse, the great Oglala leader, resisted, but he was finally captured. While trying to escape, Crazy Horse was killed by a U.S. soldier.

AFTER YOU READ

EXPLORING YOUR RESPONSES

1. There was one thing Ben wanted to change about his past–he wanted his high school diploma. Do you think it was worth his time and effort to get the diploma?

2. Nighthorse Campbell tries to learn something from defeat. How can finding out what caused a defeat help a person?

3. Ben did not try to be like other people. Why do you think some people can resist the pressure to look and act like others while other people cannot?

4. Judo helped give Nighthorse Campbell the confidence to succeed. How do you think developing a physical skill can help people excel in other areas, such as in school or a career?

5. According to Native American thinking, "art . . . is a gift you're born with." How do you think people find out what gifts they were "born with"?

UNDERSTANDING WORDS IN CONTEXT

Read the following sentences from the biography. Think about what each underlined word means. In your notebook, write what the word means as it is used in the sentence.

1. [Nighthorse Campbell's] colleagues raised their eyebrows at his cowboy hat, string tie, leather jacket, and long, graying ponytail. The House of Representatives has a dress code.

2. However, having some money was little consolation. His mother's illness and his father's frequent absences made Ben both strong and insecure.

3. Judo had given Campbell a belief in his own abilities–including the ability to rally after a loss or disappointment.

4. In this background lay the clues to his later rebelliousness. . . .
Many of his teachers liked him, though he sometimes lacked
self-discipline and wound up in detention after school.

5. This monument in Montana commemorates a battle in which
Native Americans defeated U.S. soldiers led by General
George Armstrong Custer.

RECALLING DETAILS

1. Name some of the things that made Ben's early life difficult.

2. What do some people find unusual about Nighthorse
Campbell's dress and appearance?

3. Describe the importance of judo in Campbell's life.

4. Why did the party leaders want Ben to run for the state
legislature?

5. What career led Nighthorse Campbell to explore his Native
American roots?

UNDERSTANDING INFERENCES

In your notebook, write two or three sentences from the
biography that support each of the following inferences.

1. Ben's art is important to him.

2. Nighthorse Campbell is not afraid to try new things.

3. It is never too late to complete an education.

4. Ben is proud of his Native American heritage.

5. People can learn as much from defeat as they can from victory.

INTERPRETING WHAT YOU HAVE READ

1. What do you think Ben learned from judo?

2. Why might Nighthorse Campbell's independence as a
lawmaker sometimes upset his fellow Democrats?

3. After Ben started making jewelry, he began dressing in a way that reflected his Native American heritage. Why do you think he did this?

4. Do you think Ben regrets dropping out of high school?

5. In what ways was Nighthorse Campbell's path to Congress uncommon?

ANALYZING QUOTATIONS

Read the following quotation from the biography and answer the questions below.

"You were born with a certain kind of soul in you. It's something I don't think you should imprison or hold back."

1. When Ben talks about "a certain kind of soul," what do you think he means?

2. How can a soul be "imprisoned"?

3. What might happen if a person tried to hold back his "soul"?

THINKING CRITICALLY

1. How do you think Ben was affected by his father's request *not* to tell people he was Native American?

2. Why do you think Campbell added *Nighthorse* to his name?

3. How might serving in the Air Force and training for the Olympics have affected Nighthorse Campbell's outlook on life?

4. Ben is involved in both art and politics. In what ways are these two career paths similar?

5. As a U.S. Senator, Ben Nighthorse Campbell helps make laws. If you were to write to Senator Nighthorse Campbell to suggest a law you think the country needs, what would it be and why?

SHIRLEY HILL WITT

Shirley Hill Witt (center), Akwesasne Mohawk anthropologist, par-
ticipates in a historic meeting with representatives from Somalia and
from the Navajo nation. Witt is committed to protecting human rights
and the dignity of all people, regardless of their cultural heritage.

Some students were taking notes. Others were dozing. Shirley Hill Witt was listening carefully to her anthropology[1] professor at the University of Michigan. As she listened, Shirley grew angry. The professor was complaining loudly about his students—but not about late homework or low test scores. He was complaining that there were too many women in the anthropology department! That "lecture" never left Shirley's mind. From that day on, she was committed to studying discrimination, or unfair treatment, in our society.

Shirley Hill was born in 1934, in Whittier, California. She is a member of the Akwesasne (ah-kwuh-SAHS-nee) Mohawk nation. California is a long way from the home of the Mohawk in western New York. As Shirley has found throughout her life, however, distances in miles and years can be overcome by exploration and study. As she says about her chosen field, anthropology, "I discovered that there was a discipline[2] in which one could spend all of one's time studying one's own people, and perhaps even get paid for it. I was stunned."

Anthropologists study the development of human societies. Some experts estimate[3] that there are 4,000 distinct societies in the world. Anthropologists try to discover how these societies are different and also how they are similar.

Shirley got her first taste of anthropology at 22, "quite by accident," when she was browsing through her local library. For the next few years, as Shirley and her husband moved from place

1. **anthropology** (an-throh-PAHL-uh-jee) *adj.* pertaining to the study of humans, especially their physical and cultural characteristics
2. **discipline** (DIHS-uh-plihn) *n.* branch of knowledge
3. **estimate** (EHS-tuh-mayt) *v.* to judge the approximate size, number, weight, or cost of something

to place, she would visit small towns and study the local culture. She would start her exploration by going to the local library and studying local anthropology. After a time, though, she realized that her "school on wheels" approach was impractical. If she wanted to *do* something in the field of anthropology, Witt knew she would have to get an education.

So in 1961 Shirley enrolled in a night class at a small college in Omaha, Nebraska. By this time, anthropology had turned into a passion for Witt. When she was not in class or caring for her two young children, Shirley was poking about in the basement of the local museum studying artifacts[4]–objects such as tools, pottery, and weapons. Shirley also made trips to the nearby Omaha reservation, where she observed a living, Native American, culture. With her passion came a desire to complete her college education.

In 1962, Shirley Witt left Nebraska and headed for Ann Arbor, Michigan, where she intended to enroll as a freshman at the University of Michigan. Her journey toward a degree would be a tough one because Shirley was recently divorced. Somehow, she would have to earn money and take care of her children–all while attending classes and doing homework. To make matters worse, she only had $250 left.

After making some friends and asking some questions, Witt heard that a professor, Leslie White, was looking for an assistant to help him do research. White was a well-known and highly respected anthropologist. His reputation did not scare Shirley away, however. She needed a job. Witt remembers the interview: "Professor White asked, 'What can you do?' and I replied, 'What do you want done?'" White must have liked the young woman's spirit, because for the next five years, Shirley worked closely with him while also attending classes, learning everything she could about anthropology–and more.

---

4. **artifacts** (AHRT-ih-fakts) *n. pl.* handmade objects that give clues to a culture's development

Witt's work as a research assistant for Professor White taught her about personal and professional excellence. White never cut corners. He was never slipshod.[5] She explains, "I learned more from [Professor] White about scholarship, precision,[6] organization, perseverance, and discipline than I did about anthropology, even though I learned a considerable amount of anthropology." Witt learned that sloppy work habits can mean failure as a professional. If a researcher's work is inaccurate, he or she will not be taken seriously—and could even lose a job.

The experience with Professor White paid off. Within five years, Shirley had both a bachelor's and a master's degree in anthropology. By 1969, she had earned her Ph.D. from the University of New Mexico in Albuquerque.

Throughout her years of schooling, Witt supported Native American causes, such as the National Indian Youth Council, contributed articles to Native American magazines, such as *Akwesasne Notes*, and wrote parts of books related to Native American studies. However, she did these things because she wanted to, not as part of her preparation to be an anthropologist. Witt chose to be multidisciplinary[7] in her studies rather than concentrating on a single culture. As she explains, studying her own people would have been too easy. She would have had no problem gaining access to or understanding the communities. "It just wasn't the challenge I sought," she says. (See ***Did You Know?*** on page 195 for more information about early anthropologists' studies of Native Americans.)

After earning her Ph.D., Shirley taught at the University of North Carolina, then at Colorado College. Though she enjoyed teaching, Witt was, in her heart, an activist.[8] She wanted to use

---

5. **slipshod** (SLIHP-shahd) *adj.* careless

6. **precision** (prih-SIHZH-uhn) *n.* accuracy; exactness

7. **multidisciplinary** (muhl-tih-DIHS-uh-pluh-nair-ee) *adj.* pertaining to many different fields of study

8. **activist** (AK-tuh-vihst) *n.* a person who takes positive, direct action to solve a political or social problem

her knowledge to stop the injustice she had seen while studying various cultures. As she says, "By 1974 I had already worked with blacks in Omaha, Chicanos in New Mexico, and poor whites and blacks in Appalachia, to say nothing of [my] involvement in Indian affairs aside from anthropological research." Witt often spoke publicly about injustice, and by 1975, she was a well-known speaker and writer in the women's rights movement.

That same year, Witt received a call from the United States Commission on Civil Rights (USCCR). Her activities in civil rights had brought her to the commission's attention. The USCCR is responsible for seeing that the civil rights of people in the United States are protected. It investigates suspected cases of discrimination—particularly ones in which many people are affected. Shirley Witt's background in anthropology and her Native American ancestry gave her a valuable perspective on discrimination.

Witt moved to Denver, Colorado, and became the director of the Rocky Mountain Regional Office of the USCCR. There, she and her team of professionals concerned themselves with large-scale discrimination. For example, in Utah they studied whether women were having more difficulty obtaining credit[9] than men were. In South Dakota, they investigated whether Native Americans were receiving the same sentences for crimes and getting the same quality legal representation as non-Native Americans were.

Shirley Witt's team included anthropologists, social scientists, lawyers, and writers. Their work required months—and sometimes years—of research. Often, they had to carefully read long reports and records to uncover a pattern of abuse. Usually they were required to prove that an entire group was being discriminated against—not just one or two people. When the team's reports were finished, the results were sent to a number

9. **credit** (KREHD-iht) *n.* the ability to borrow money

of people, including the President and members of the U.S. Congress.

Over the years, Witt has also been involved with such organizations as the Indian Rights Committee, the Federal Women's Program Committee, the National Association of Human Rights Workers, and the National Women's Political Caucus. On a more personal level, Witt has written 4 books and over 60 articles, stories, and poems that reflect her interest in the Native and Latino Americans of the Southwest.

Shirley Witt's career has a definite theme: the protection of human rights and human dignity. She has worked among the poor and powerless and the rich and powerful. For Witt, every person, no matter what his or her condition in life, has rights that must be protected. "The path of my life has taken me through human situations which have left me with an undeniable need to participate in matters concerning civil–human–rights." As she travels this path, Shirley Hill Witt is working for all of us.

> **Did You Know?** Shirley Hill Witt has found some early discussions of Native American culture to be inaccurate and misleading. In her words, "so much of the descriptive literature about Indians was such nonsense that one could spend a lifetime redoing it . . . [for example] 'the passion of love was unknown among the Iroquois' or 'the Hopi ran 40 miles to their fields each day' and 'the Indian women were slaves, the men lords.'" From this sample of what some anthropologists have written, it is clear why careful, accurate research is so important.

AFTER YOU READ

EXPLORING YOUR RESPONSES

1. If you were in Shirley Witt's class at the University of Michigan, how might you have reacted to the professor's complaints?

2. While Witt was taking her first anthropology class, she would study artifacts in local museums. What do you think you could learn from studying the artifacts of a culture?

3. If you could travel around the United States to study a subject, what would it be? Explain.

4. What role do you think education plays in preventing discrimination?

5. Imagine that an anthropologist from another planet landed on earth and said to you, "I see you have some problems with discrimination in your society. Why?" How would you answer?

UNDERSTANDING WORDS IN CONTEXT

Read the following sentences from the biography. Think about what each underlined word means. In your notebook, write what the word means as it is used in the sentence.

1. Shirley was poking about in the basement of the local museum studying artifacts—objects such as tools, pottery, and weapons.

2. White never cut corners. He was never slipshod.

3. Though she enjoyed teaching, Witt was, in her heart, an activist. She wanted to use her knowledge to stop the injustice she had seen while studying various cultures.

4. As she says about her chosen field, anthropology, "I discovered that there was a discipline in which one could spend all of one's time studying one's own people."

5. Some experts <u>estimate</u> that there are 4,000 distinct societies in the world.

RECALLING DETAILS

1. How did Witt begin exploring the field of anthropology?
2. What skills did Shirley Witt learn from Professor White?
3. Why did Witt leave teaching in 1975?
4. While working for the United States Commission on Civil Rights, what did Witt and her team do?
5. Why did Witt decide not to specialize in Native American anthropology?

UNDERSTANDING INFERENCES

In your notebook, write two or three sentences from the biography that support each of the following inferences.

1. Shirley Witt believes in both "learning by doing" and formal education.
2. It is not always easy to prove that discrimination has taken place.
3. Witt put the research skills she learned in college to use later in her life.
4. Witt thinks people should be treated fairly.
5. Witt does not give up when things are tough.

INTERPRETING WHAT YOU HAVE READ

1. What effect did working with Professor Leslie White have on Witt?
2. When Professor White asked Witt, "What can you do?", she replied, "What do you want done?" What does this tell you about Witt?
3. Why did Witt decide to go to school, rather than study on her own?

4. How might having two small children to raise have affected Witt's educational and career choices?

5. Why is accuracy so important in anthropology?

ANALYZING QUOTATIONS

Read the following quotation from the biography and answer the questions below.

"The path of my life has taken me through human situations which have left me with an undeniable need to participate in matters concerning civil–human–rights."

1. What sort of "human situations" do you think Witt is talking about?

2. What are some of the rights we all have as human beings?

3. Which human rights do you think need protection now? Why?

THINKING CRITICALLY

1. When Witt first discovered anthropology, she liked it because it allowed a person to "study one's own people." Later she chose not to concentrate on Native American studies. Why do you think she changed her mind?

2. Although Witt had little money and two children to support, she still went to college. Why do you think she was so determined?

3. In Witt's job with the Commission on Civil Rights, she spent long hours doing research. Why do you think such research is necessary?

4. How does Professor White's lesson—never do a job half-way—apply to careers outside of anthropology?

5. The theme of Witt's career can be stated as "the protection of human rights and human dignity." If someone were to write your biography 30 years from now, what would you like your "theme" to be?

THOMAS SEGUNDO

Thomas Segundo, Tohono O'Odham council chairman, became the youngest Native American leader in the United States at age 26. Under his leadership, the council passed laws that improved the lives and community of the Tohono O'Odham people.

In 1946, Thomas Segundo (say-GUHN-doh) took a vacation from which he never returned. The place he visited was suffering from a terrible drought. Cattle and other farm animals were dying because of the lack of water. Horses had to be killed because there was no food to feed them. A hot wind blew constantly and the topsoil of the farmland was blowing away in brown clouds. The people living in this place had little hope that their lives would ever be better.

So, why did Tom Segundo go to this place and stay? The reason was simple. This place was his home—the Papago (pah-puh-GOH) Reservation in Arizona. (The Papago now call themselves the Tohono O'Odham [toh-HOH-noh AH-AHD-uhm]. See **Did You Know?** on page 204 for more information on the Papago's decision to change their name.) Now that he had returned after a long time away, Segundo realized that his people needed him.

Tom was born on the reservation in 1920, but he left as a young man to go to school. Eventually, he moved to San Francisco and got a job in the ship-building industry. He showed talent and initiative,[1] and quickly became a supervisor in his company. Tom had plans to go to the University of California to get a degree in engineering. But, before pursuing his education, he took a vacation to visit friends and family on the reservation.

Segundo soon realized that the people living on the reservation were facing a desperate situation and needed help. Even though he was on vacation, he set to work. He borrowed a truck to haul food for the animals. The roads were so bad that he was changing tires every day.

---

1. **initiative** (ih-NIHSH-uh-tihv) *n.* responsibility for taking the first step; ability to act independently

While he was hauling food, Tom heard that an old friend was looking for him. The friend was a road engineer who worked on the reservation. He came to visit, and, as they caught up on old times, the engineer asked Segundo to become his assistant. At first, Tom hesitated. He still planned to return to San Francisco after his vacation. But then he took the job, thinking that if he did not like it, he could always go back to California.

As Tom traveled the reservation on his new job, he was appalled[2] by the poverty he saw and how it was affecting the Tohono O'Odham. World War II had just ended. Many of the young Native Americans who had fought in the war now were returning home. But there were few jobs for them. Like many veterans,[3] they were only trained for military work. As a result, some of them started drinking and getting into fights. Segundo decided to do something about that.

Tom's solution was to organize a football team. But first, he needed money for equipment. Segundo went to the Tohono O'Odham council, which governed the reservation, for help. At first, council members refused to get involved. After all, from their perspective, the young people on the reservation were nothing but troublemakers. But Segundo would not relent.[4] Finally, the council agreed to loan him $150.

The football team was a huge success. It was undefeated in its first season. With the money earned from ticket sales, Segundo was able to pay back the $150 and buy more equipment. Perhaps the team was not the answer to every problem, but it gave people a feeling of pride in their community—an important step.

People were beginning to notice Tom Segundo. He seemed always to be organizing or participating in some event. Before long, Segundo was being mentioned as a possible chairman of the Tohono O'Odham council. Tom doubted that he had the

---

2. **appalled** (uh-PAWLD) *v.* filled with shock or horror

3. **veterans** (VEHT-uhr-uhnz) *n. pl.* people who have served in the armed forces

4. **relent** (rih-LEHNT) *v.* become more agreeable, less stubborn

qualifications[5] for the position. After much coaxing, however, he was persuaded to run in the election.

Probably no one was more surprised than Tom Segundo when the votes were counted. At 26, he was elected by a landslide and became the youngest elected Native American leader in the United States.

The first problem Tom Segundo had to solve as chairman was the Tohono O'Odham's lack of money. Though it was the second largest tribe in Arizona, the Tohono O'Odham were desperately poor. Many people who were not Native Americans had profitable businesses on the large reservation. However, these business people did not pay taxes to the Tohono O'Odham as they would to other communities. It is by taxing businesses and individuals that communities get money to pay for schools, roads, and other services. Tom immediately saw how unfair this situation was to his people.

One of the first things Segundo did as chairman was to pass a business tax law. At first, the business people protested and said they would not pay. One trader even tried to bribe[6] Segundo so he would "change his mind" about the tax. Tom stood his ground. The businesses then threatened to complain to the governor of Arizona and the U.S. Congress if necessary. Tom explains, "They [the business people] seemed to overlook the fact that this is a reservation, not a concentration camp and the only way anyone can come on the reservation and establish a business is by permission of the tribe. It's a privilege." In a few months, the taxes were being paid.

Next, Tom took on the lumber business in his community. For many years outside lumber traders had driven into the forested areas of the Tohono O'Odham Reservation and loaded

---

5. **qualifications** (kwawl-ih-fih-KAY-shuhnz) *n. pl.* knowledge, skills, or experience that enable someone to do a job

6. **bribe** (BREYEB) *v.* offer money or favors to get someone to do something illegal

large trucks with cut timber without paying for it. Tom was determined to stop this. First, the council passed a law that made it illegal for outsiders to cut reservation lumber without permission. Then Segundo charged the lumber businesses a tax for cutting timber and using reservation roads.

Segundo's efforts paid off. Soon, with the money earned from the taxes, the Tohono O'Odham were able to take care of some of the problems on the reservation. Until then, Tom had been working as a road engineer during the day and as chairman during the evening and on weekends. With money finally coming in, he was able to stop working two jobs. Segundo could receive a small salary and devote all his time to the community.

The Tohono O'Odham community was once more full of energy and ideas about making things better. No more did people have to go to the non–Native American official at the Bureau of Indian Affairs with their concerns and dreams. Now, even though they had to travel a great distance, the Tohono O'Odham went to Tom Segundo and the council with their concerns.

Like any great leader, Tom Segundo had a vision for his people. But visions need a "backbone" and details. So for almost one year, he visited every one of the 73 villages on the reservation to ask questions and to discuss ideas. Segundo then put all he had learned into a long-range plan. The plan included ways to conserve the land, bring more water for crops, educate the children, and improve health care services. Because so many people had been involved in developing the plan, it was well understood and supported. The council passed it unanimously.

For the next 20 years Tom Segundo worked to put the plan into action. He was re-elected council chairman seven times. After his seventh term, Segundo went to the University of Chicago to take classes in law and government so he could better lead his people. He believed that the education would help him as a negotiator[7] in Washington, D.C., where he often traveled to

---

7. **negotiator** (nih-GOH-shee-ayt-uhr) *n.* a person who discusses issues and tries to bring people into agreement

work out agreements with government officials. Tom, however, would not live to see all of his dreams become a reality. In 1971, he was killed in an airplane crash. He was 51 years old.

When Tom Segundo died, the reservation that mourned his death was very different from the one he had visited almost 30 years before on his vacation. One man's love, vision, and toughness had changed the world of the Tohono O'Odham forever.

> *Did You Know? In the 1500s Spanish explorers gave the Tohono O'Odham the name "Papago," which means "bean eaters," because beans were the Tohono O'Odham's main crop. As was true for many Native American nations, the name given to them by European explorers stuck. After centuries of being known as the Papago, however, the Tohono O'Odham voted in the 1980s to officially change their name to the term they had always used for themselves. In their language, "Tohono O'Odham" means "desert people."*

AFTER YOU READ

EXPLORING YOUR RESPONSES

1. Thomas Segundo began helping the people of the Tohono O'Odham reservation in "small ways." Why do you think small acts of kindness sometimes mean more than big "heroic" acts?

2. Segundo noticed that some of the young men on the reservation were getting into trouble because they had no job. How might unemployment lead to trouble?

3. The people on the reservation looked up to Tom Segundo as a leader. Whom do you think of as a leader and why?

4. Segundo chose football as a way of raising people's spirits. In what ways do sports bring people together?

5. Segundo not only gave his community hope for a better life, but he made that better life happen. Think of something you hope for. What might you do to make it happen?

UNDERSTANDING WORDS IN CONTEXT

Read the following sentences from the biography. Think about what each underlined word means. In your notebook, write what the word means as it is used in the sentence.

1. He showed talent and initiative, and quickly became a supervisor in his company.

2. As Tom traveled the reservation on his new job, he was appalled by the poverty he saw and how it was affecting the Tohono O'Odham.

3. But Segundo would not relent. Finally, the council agreed to loan him $150.

4. One trader even tried to bribe Segundo so he would "change his mind" about the tax.

5. He believed that the education would help him as a <u>negotiator</u> in Washington, D.C., where he often traveled to <u>work out</u> agreements with government officials.

RECALLING DETAILS

1. Why did Segundo decide to stay on the reservation?
2. Describe the conditions on the Papago Reservation in 1946.
3. What did Segundo do to help the veterans feel better about themselves?
4. How did Segundo and the council solve the community's money problem?
5. How did Segundo prepare the Tohono O'Odham long-range plan?

UNDERSTANDING INFERENCES

In your notebook, write two or three sentences from the biography that support each of the following inferences.

1. Segundo had creative ideas about government.
2. Many problems can be solved with strong leadership.
3. Segundo was not afraid of powerful people.
4. Segundo valued the opinions and concerns of his people.
5. Tom Segundo was popular.

INTERPRETING WHAT YOU HAVE READ

1. What did Segundo hope to accomplish by forming a football team on the reservation?
2. At first, the council was reluctant to loan Segundo money for the football team. Besides being annoyed with the troublemakers, why might the council have been reluctant?
3. At 26, Segundo was elected chairman "by a landslide." Why do you think people had such confidence in Segundo's leadership abilities?

4. How were the taxes that Segundo established able to help the Tohono O'Odham community?

5. Tom Segundo had a vision for his people. What do you think this vision was?

ANALYZING QUOTATIONS

Read the following quotation from the biography and answer the questions below.

> *"The only way anyone can come on the reservation and establish a business is by permission of the tribe. It's a privilege."*

1. What does Segundo mean by saying people need "permission of the tribe" to do business on the reservation?

2. How is Segundo's opinion in this quote different from the attitude he found when he first returned to the reservation?

3. Suppose that someone borrowed your jacket, rode your bike, or planted a garden in your yard without asking your permission. Would they have the right to do so? How would you react?

THINKING CRITICALLY

1. Why do you think many of the Tohono O'Odham people chose to stay on the reservation despite its poor conditions?

2. Why would the ability to negotiate be useful to a Native American official?

3. In what way did taxing people who did business on the reservation help the Tohono O'Odham feel more secure about their ability to govern themselves?

4. Why did Segundo spend a year working on a plan when he could have just passed some laws right away?

5. If you were in Tom Segundo's place, would you have stayed on the reservation or gone back to San Francisco? Explain.

LAURA WATERMAN WITTSTOCK

Laura Waterman Wittstock, Seneca media consultant, is shown here with her granddaughter Candice Big Eagle. Wittstock works to ensure that Native Americans are represented fairly by the press.

Laura Waterman's mother tended the long rows of tomatoes, beans, and corn with care. The garden was just behind their home on the Cattaraugus (kat-ah-RAW-guhs) Reservation, in western New York. Each year, Mrs. Waterman harvested the ripe vegetables and fruits, which grew in abundance.[1] What the family did not eat right away, she preserved for the winter.

Laura's family had many relatives in the area. Almost always, they returned home with gifts of preserved vegetables or maybe some fresh eggs from the Wittstocks' chickens. As a child, Laura was not surprised by the gifts of food—her mother had a generous nature. When Laura grew older, however, she realized that there was more behind the gifts than generosity. Many of her relatives depended on this food to survive during the hard economic times of the 1930s.

Helping others and "sticking together" were traditions in Laura's family—ones she never forgot. As an adult, Laura Waterman Wittstock has carried on this tradition, but Laura's gifts are in the form of words, rather than vegetables. She uses her energy, knowledge, and writing talent to help her people preserve their heritage and expand their opportunities.

Laura was born in 1937 on the Cattaraugus Reservation. Her parents were both Seneca (SEHN-ih-kuh), a nation of Native Americans who once lived between the Genesee River and Seneca Lake in what is now New York State. Laura's family name, Waterman, is English. Early English explorers had given a group of Senecas this name because of the skillful way in which they maneuvered[2] their canoes through the waterways. As a

1. **abundance** (uh-BUN-duhns) *n.* a great amount
2. **maneuvered** (muh-NOO-vuhrd) *v.* guided with skill

child, Laura learned about Seneca history and culture. "I was taught by my clan,[3] my family members' contributions, and I learned from both my parents that happiness came from helping others." (See *Did You Know?* on page 212 for more information on Seneca clans.)

Laura was the youngest of five children, and the only girl. She recalls her early childhood with fondness. "My father did not treat me like a little child. He [often] talked to me about things I didn't understand, but I was very eager to listen to his stories. . . . [He] knew how to tell funny stories and make me feel like I was hearing grown-up conversation."

When Laura was still a girl, the Watermans moved to Buffalo, New York. It was a difficult move for her. For the first time, her classmates were not Native American. Making friends was not as easy as it had been on the reservation. A brother, who lived in Hawaii, invited Laura to live with him when she was still in elementary school. Laura's mother agreed, and for nine years, Laura lived in Hawaii.

Hawaii was very different from western New York. Yet Laura Waterman adapted[4]–she learned to appreciate the special beauty of the islands. She remembers, "There was no snow, no fall when the leaves would turn brilliant colors, and no spring when the creeks would run high and wild along the banks. I missed my parents very much. . . . [But] I learned to swim as fast as the other children. I learned the names of the many plants, animals, fish, and birds, and I learned some of the stories about old Hawaii and how the Native people first went there to live. So, even though I returned to my own Native roots, I will always know that Hawaii is also a part of my own growing up, too."

Later, Laura Waterman married and moved to Minnesota. There, she started a very successful career in communications– the information business, which includes newspapers, magazines,

---

3. **clan** (KLAN) *n.* a group of people who have a common ancestor and common interests
4. **adapted** (uh-DAPT-uhd) *v.* adjusted to new conditions

TV, and radio. Wittstock's goal for more than 20 years has been to ensure[5] that Native Americans are represented fairly by the media. More than that, she has worked to develop Native American newspapers and radio and TV programs. She began by improving conditions for Native American reporters.

While attending a Congressional press conference in the early 1970s, Laura encountered[6] discrimination firsthand, when she and other Native American reporters were denied seats. This practice was not unusual. To those arranging the press conferences, the Native Americans were not considered "important" enough. Only after people like Wittstock complained were the Native American reporters given the same access[7] as other journalists were.

Laura did not stop her fight for equality after this victory, however. For 20 years she has done whatever she can to prove that Native and non-Native American newspapers are equally important. As she says, "The native press of North America has had a long history. Most of those presses were either destroyed or withered because of opposition." Wittstock has worked hard to build these presses again because, to her, the media represents the path to the future. She explains, "What we're trying to do now is to get the attention of the [leaders] of the various tribes and nations and to plead our case with them that a free press and an adequate press are important for the future of the Indian people."

How has Laura's career reflected her concerns? From 1977 to 1984, Laura Wittstock was chair of the board of MIGIZI Communications. *Migizi* means "eagle" in Ojibwe (oh-JIHB-wuh). This company produces radio and TV news programs of interest to both Native and non-Native Americans in Minnesota. These programs are beamed by satellite to 17 radio and television stations in the Great Lakes region. Besides producing its own

---

5. **ensure** (ihn-SHOOR) *v.* to make sure or certain

6. **encountered** (ehn-KOWN-tuhrd) *v.* met unexpectedly; came upon

7. **access** (AK-sehs) *n.* the right to enter or approach

shows, MIGIZI offers classes in journalism and broadcasting, giving young Native Americans an opportunity to "break into" the media. Wittstock became MIGIZI's president in 1985.

Wittstock has also served as the director of the American Indian Press Association. The purpose of this organization is to help Native American communities develop their own newspapers and to fight for the rights of Native American journalists. For many years, Laura was a journalist, writing a monthly report on laws affecting Native Americans. Her work allowed Native American communities to keep track of the many laws and regulations that affected them. In 1992, Laura was honored for her contributions with a Human Rights Award, given by the Minnesota Lawyers International Human Rights Committee.

If you were to paint a picture of Laura Wittstock's life, however, her work in the media would cover only one part of the canvas. She has made many other contributions to her community. Some of the issues she cares most about include alcoholism, women's rights, and children's education. She uses her writing and programming skills to draw attention to these issues.

Besides reporting news and writing a regular column for *The Alley*, a Minneapolis newspaper, Laura writes fiction and nonfiction. In 1993, her book *Sugarbush: Ojibwe Maple Sugar Making* was published. It teaches children how the Ojibwe people of Minnesota make sugar. Like the vegetables from her mother's garden long ago, this book is one of Laura Waterman Wittstock's gifts to others.

Did You Know? *The Seneca, along with five other Native American groups, belong to the Iroquois (IHR-uh-kwoi) league called Six Nations. Their society is a system of clans, or groups of people with a common ancestor. Each clan is headed by a woman. The clan* into which Laura Waterman was born is called the Heron. An ancestor on her mother's side was the great Seneca hero Cornplanter. In the late 1700s, the new U.S. government set out to destroy the Seneca, in part, because they had sided with the British during the American Revolution. Cornplanter led the fight to save Seneca land and culture. Cornplanter's brother, Handsome Lake, was an important religious leader who urged his people to reject "white ways." Wittstock's mother was born on land that once belonged to Cornplanter.

AFTER YOU READ

EXPLORING YOUR RESPONSES

1. Adjusting to life in Buffalo was difficult for Wittstock. Why is it sometimes difficult to adjust to a new situation?

2. The Wittstock family had a tradition of helping others. How might family traditions affect people as they grow up?

3. Wittstock recognizes the power of the media. How much influence do you think the media has in shaping people's ideas and opinions?

4. Wittstock thinks it is important for Native American communities to keep track of the laws and regulations that affect them. How does knowing, or not knowing, the rules of your school affect you and other students?

5. MIGIZI gives Native Americans the opportunity to produce programs that interest their community. If you could produce your own radio or TV show, what would it be about and why?

UNDERSTANDING WORDS IN CONTEXT

Read the following sentences from the biography. Think about what each underlined word means. In your notebook, write what the word means as it is used in the sentence.

1. Each year, Mrs. Waterman harvested the ripe vegetables and fruits, which grew in underlined abundance. What the family did not eat right away, she preserved.

2. Early English explorers had given a group of Senecas [the name Waterman] because of the skillful way in which they maneuvered their canoes through the waterways.

3. Hawaii was very different from western New York. Yet Laura Waterman adapted—she learned to appreciate the special beauty of the islands.

4. While attending a Congressional press conference in the early 1970s, Laura <u>encountered</u> discrimination firsthand, when she and other Native American reporters were denied seats.

5. Only after people like Wittstock complained were Native American reporters given the same <u>access</u> as other journalists were.

RECALLING DETAILS

1. Why did Laura go to Hawaii?

2. Why did Laura's mother give gifts of food to relatives?

3. Describe Laura's experience at the Congressional press conference she attended in the early 1970s.

4. How does MIGIZI help young Native Americans break into broadcasting?

5. Why did Wittstock receive the Human Rights award?

UNDERSTANDING INFERENCES

In your notebook, write two or three sentences from the biography that support each of the following inferences.

1. Wittstock was influenced by the traditions of her family.

2. Adjusting to a new home can be both difficult and exciting.

3. Wittstock is concerned about protecting the rights of Native Americans.

4. Wittstock is a leader.

5. Wittstock wants to help her community.

INTERPRETING WHAT YOU HAVE READ

1. How is a "free press" important to the future of Native Americans?

2. Why do you think Wittstock chose a career in the media?

3. What effect did attending the Congressional press conference in the 1970s have on Wittstock?

4. Why did Wittstock become director of the American Indian Press Association?

5. How does MIGIZI help Native Americans?

ANALYZING QUOTATIONS

Read the following quotation from the biography and answer the questions below.

"I was taught by my clan, my family members' contributions, and I learned from both my parents that happiness came from helping others."

1. What sort of contributions do you think Wittstock means?

2. How do people learn from the contributions of others?

3. What lessons can a person's clan teach?

THINKING CRITICALLY

1. Laura Waterman Wittstock has worked to ensure that Native American reporters are not viewed as less important than other reporters. Why do you think this issue is so important to her?

2. How is Wittstock like her mother?

3. Wittstock says that Native American presses were "either destroyed or withered because of opposition." Why do you think people might be opposed to these newspapers?

4. Wittstock thinks a "free and adequate press is important for the future of the Indian people." Do you agree with her? Why or why not?

5. Laura Waterman Wittstock has kept alive her family tradition of helping others. What kinds of family traditions do you think should be carried on? Why?

BILLY FRANK

Billy Frank, Nisqually environmental activist, has worked to protect
the fishing rights of his people. Frank's ancestors not only depended on
salmon for nourishment, but also saw the fish as a powerful life force.

It was a birthday Billy Frank would never forget. He turned 33 that day in 1964 and planned to spend the day doing what he liked best—fishing. As usual, Frank headed for his favorite spot along the Nisqually (nihs-KWAH-lee) River—the same spot he and his father had fished for years. In fact, Frank's Nisqually ancestors had fished for the salmon in this river for thousands of years.

On this day, however, Billy Frank would not do much fishing. No sooner had he put his line into the river than state officials zoomed up to arrest him. He left peacefully. This happened almost every time he went fishing, though he often had time to catch a few fish before leaving.

Billy Frank was born in 1931 on the Nisqually Reservation, south of Tacoma, Washington. By the 1930s, however, the Nisqually had little control over their land or its resources,[1] like the salmon. They had also lost control, many years back, of so basic a right as naming themselves. Billy's name comes from his grandfather, who worked for a rancher named Frank. Non-Native Americans called his grandfather "Frank's Indian," and then "Indian Frank." When Billy's father attended a Catholic boarding school, the priests there gave him the name Billy Frank. Though Billy uses this name given his father, he is proud of his Nisqually name, Qu-Lash-Qud. The small town where Billy grew up and lives today is called Frank's Landing, after his father.

Billy's father, who lived to be 104 years old, often told Billy that when the salmon were gone, their people would also pass away. Billy explains the importance of the river and his land, "An Indian needs his river, his mountain, wherever he prays, so when he comes back from wherever he's been, there's a place to go. At

---

1. **resources** (REE-sohrs-uhs) *n. pl.* natural sources of wealth

least I have a river I can sit by. A lot of Indians don't have a river." For many years, however, it seemed Billy Frank did not have even that.

Even before his arrest in 1964, Billy Frank had begun to fight for the salmon. To most Native Americans living in the Pacific Northwest, salmon and fishing are more than a way to earn a living. They have cultural significance[2] as well. Thousands of years ago, Native Americans were attracted to the region because of the great number of salmon. Communities were built near the salmon's spawning[3] grounds. People dried and smoked the salmon so it could be eaten all year long. But the salmon were also revered.[4] These early Native Americans saw salmon as a powerful life force, and they honored the salmon in their art and legends.

In 1854, Frank's Nisqually ancestors signed a treaty[5] with the U.S. government selling 2.2 million acres of their land, and the right to fish in its rivers and streams. Almost immediately, however, Native Americans began to question the many treaties their leaders were signing. Had they been tricked or forced into signing? Were Native Americans getting what the treaties promised?

By the 1970s, Billy Frank and other Native Americans, many of whom were lawyers, were trying to overturn[6] some of the treaties signed in the 1800s. Often the lawyers found mistakes in these documents, as well as promises to Native Americans that had not been fulfilled. They were determined to use the system that had worked against them in the past to obtain the lands and rights that were lawfully theirs. (See *Did You Know?* on page 222 for more information on these treaties.)

---

2. **significance** (sihg-NIHF-uh-kuhns) *n.* importance
3. **spawning** (SPAWN-ihng) *adj.* places where eggs are laid
4. **revered** (rih-VIHRD) *v.* regarded with deep respect
5. **treaty** (TREE-tee) *n.* an agreement or contract
6. **overturn** (oh-vuhr-TURN) *v.* to defeat or reverse

For many years, Washington State had controlled the right to fish salmon in the region. The state determined at what time of the year the salmon could be fished. By requiring that people have permission from the state (a fishing license) in order to fish, the state also controlled who could fish for salmon. In an effort to regain control of the fishing rights, Frank read the Medicine Creek Treaty, signed by his ancestors in 1854, very carefully. In the treaty, the U.S. government promised his ancestors fishing rights in the very places he was being arrested! This document helped Billy regain control of his ancestors' land and river and of the fish that lived in it.

Frank's most powerful weapon was the "fish-in," which he started using in the 1950s. Often accompanied by his father, he would go to the Nisqually River and fish, even though it was not permitted. Game wardens would then arrest them. Sometimes non–Native Americans would attack the Franks, angry that they were fishing when others were not allowed to fish. "When I think of all the days I got beat up, I can remember what my dad said, that these people are trying to kill us, but we got through it. We did. We did!" The protests attracted attention, and sometimes celebrities, such as actor Marlon Brando, would join the fish-ins.

It was during these protests that the strength of Billy Frank's character emerged. Like all true leaders, he had the patience and determination to keep struggling for his beliefs. "I never gave up. Getting beat up, my tires slashed, shot at, arrested, cursed, cussed, spit on. You name it. I still don't hate anyone." By the time he was 43 years old, Billy Frank had been arrested more than 50 times for protesting.

In 1974, Billy Frank's efforts finally paid off. The fish-ins and protests forced state and federal officials to review the old treaties. In one case, a federal judge concluded that the 25 Native American groups of coastal Washington are entitled to 50 percent of the region's annual salmon catch. The decision returned control of valuable resources to the Nisqually people.

Billy Frank did not stop trying to improve life for his people after the 1974 court decision. As he points out, lawsuits will not make more salmon. To protect the fish and the Nisqually way of life, Billy lobbied[7] government agencies for various environmental laws. He has worked for conservation of water and other natural resources. Often he has angered people, including the logging industry, by asking that limits be set on what people can take from the area. Frank also has helped bring back the bald eagle population by pushing through laws that control the use of pesticides.[8] These chemicals kill bugs that can harm plants and trees, but they can also harm other animals, such as bald eagles, that live in the areas that are sprayed.

You might think that Frank would refuse to work with the people who had arrested, and sometimes beaten, him. However, Frank understands that change comes through cooperation. He believes that people with opposing ideas can work together. He calls his approach "cooperative management," and the secret is listening to and respecting other points of view. His strategy is being used in other states where disputes about the use of natural resources occur.

Frank uses cooperative management every day in his job as chairperson of the Northwest Indian Fisheries Commission. This organization represents the interests of 20 Washington Native American groups in dealing with state and federal agencies. It is not hard to pick Billy out in meetings with politicians and business people. He is the one with the silvery ponytail, cowboy boots, blue jeans, and plaid work shirt. People who know him say he is warm and self-assured—someone who is at peace with himself.

Billy continues to fight—not just for the Nisqually but for people everywhere—because the environment touches everyone's life. "You never do anything alone. We've got to start looking to the future to make sure our people have the energy to continue

---

7. **lobbied** (LAHB-eed) *v.* tried to influence or convince
8. **pesticides** (PEHS-tuh-seyedz) *n. pl.* chemicals used to destroy pests

on. I see all those little children running around and say: 'We've got to do it for the next generation and the generation after that.'"

In 1992, Billy Frank received the Albert Schweitzer (SHVEYET-suhr) Award for service to the human community. Among the other people who have won the award is former President Jimmy Carter. "We're running behind in protecting the resources in our country. We've just got to do more to make people understand that the economy can be balanced with resources. We don't have to take the last tree or the last drop of water. We have to talk. . . . We have to give a little, all of us. Thank goodness there are more good people than bad people in this country."

> ***Did You Know?*** *Between 1853 and 1857, Congress ratified 52 treaties by which Native American groups living in Idaho, Oregon, and Washington lost 157 million acres. Why did Native Americans sign these treaties? Often, they believed that the agreements would bring peace and encourage friendly relations with the United States. At other times, they did not understand the documents they were signing because they did not speak or read English.*
>
> *Today, English is no longer a barrier. Frank appreciates the support he receives from young, college-educated leaders. As he says, "I see the leadership in these young women who are coming up, as well as the younger men, that wasn't there before as far as the professionalism and policy direction they give. It makes me feel good to know this movement will continue."*

AFTER YOU READ

EXPLORING YOUR RESPONSES

1. Billy Frank has two names: the Nisqually name his parents gave him and the English name the priests at the boarding school gave his father. How important do you think a person's name is? Explain.

2. Billy Frank and his father often worked together. Describe a project you would like to work on with an adult.

3. Native Americans have been promised many things they have not received. If this happened to you, how would you go about getting what was rightfully yours?

4. Billy tried for many years to regain control of fishing rights. What problem do you think is worth spending many years trying to solve?

5. The salmon is sacred to the Nisqually and appears in much of their art. If you were to use an animal as a symbol for your culture group, what would it be and why?

UNDERSTANDING WORDS IN CONTEXT

Read the following sentences from the biography. Think about what each underlined word means. In your notebook, write what the word means as it is used in the sentence.

1. To most Native Americans living in the Pacific Northwest, salmon and fishing are more than a way to earn a living. They have cultural significance as well.

2. People dried and smoked the salmon so it could be eaten all year long. But the salmon were also revered. These early Native Americans saw salmon as a powerful life force.

3. In 1854, Frank's Nisqually ancestors signed a treaty with the U.S. government selling 2.2 million acres of their land.

4. By the 1970s, Billy Frank and other Native Americans, many

of whom were lawyers, were trying to <u>overturn</u> some of the treaties signed in the 1800s.

5. To protect the fish and the Nisqually way of life, Billy <u>lobbied</u> government agencies for various environmental laws.

RECALLING DETAILS

1. What happened on Billy Frank's birthday in 1964?
2. How did Billy Frank's grandfather get his name?
3. What environmental concerns does Frank have?
4. What did Billy discover when he read the Medicine Lodge Treaty of 1854?
5. What is a fish-in?

UNDERSTANDING INFERENCES

In your notebook, write two or three sentences from the biography that support each of the following inferences.

1. Billy Frank believes in settling differences by talking and listening.
2. The salmon is more than a source of food to the Nisqually.
3. Billy can be persistent.
4. Native Americans have learned to fight within the system to protect their rights.
5. Billy Frank's hard work has been recognized.

INTERPRETING WHAT YOU READ

1. Why do you think Billy Frank chose a fish-in rather than some other form of protest?
2. Frank's father believed that if the salmon were destroyed, the Nisqually would be destroyed, too. In what sense would destroying the salmon "kill" the Nisqually?
3. Why do you think studying treaties became an important strategy for Native American activists in the 1970s?

4. Frank says "You never do anything alone." What do you think he means by this?

5. Why do you think Frank refused to become bitter about the way state game officials treated him?

ANALYZING QUOTATIONS

Read the following quotation from the biography and answer the questions below.

> "We have to talk. . . . We have to give a little, all of us. Thank goodness there are more good people than bad people in this country."

1. Why is "giving a little" important to settling a problem?

2. Do you agree that there are "more good people than bad people in this country"? Explain.

3. Think of a time when you have used the "give-and-take" appoach to settle a problem. How would you approach the problem now, after reading this biography?

THINKING CRITICALLY

1. How are cooperative management and fish-ins similar? How are they different?

2. Respect seems to be one of Frank's basic values. What does he respect? Explain.

3. Many of the treaties that were signed long ago are now being re-examined. Do you think it is right to undo what has already been done? Explain your position.

4. Why do you think Native Americans today—who do not need to fish for salmon to survive—still feel strongly about their fishing rights?

5. Billy Frank has been honored with the Albert Schweitzer Award for his many contributions to our nation. If you were to receive an honor at some time in your life, what contribution would you want to be recognized for and why?

CULTURAL CONNECTIONS

Thinking About What People Do

1. Imagine that you and your family have directly benefited from the work of one of the people in this unit. Write a thank-you note to that person. Be sure to mention the ways he or she has helped you.

2. Imagine that you and a partner have been asked to create a collage that shows what one of the people in this unit has accomplished. Make the collage using pictures from magazines and other available sources, or draw your own illustrations of the person's accomplishments.

3. Pretend that two of the people in this unit are meeting for the first time. With a partner, write a short dialogue in which the people describe to each other the issues that are important to them and the ways they support these issues.

Thinking About Culture

1. How were some of the people in this unit influenced by family members as they grew up or chose their life's work? Give three examples.

2. List some ways in which one person in this unit has protected the rights of others. What in this person's background made him or her want to fight for these rights?

3. According to Shirley Hill Witt, some anthropologists have written inaccurate descriptions of Native American cultures. Why is accuracy important? What might be some reasons for the inaccuracies?

Building Research Skills

Work with one or two partners to complete the following activity.

Some of the people discussed in this unit have worked to change laws that affect Native Americans or to reinterpret treaties that were made many years ago between the U.S. government and Native Americans. Make a list of questions you would like to answer about these laws. Your questions might include:

Hint: The Bibliography at the back of this book will give you a list of books and articles that can help you start your research.

☆ What laws were passed in the last 20 years that have affected Native Americans?

☆ How have these laws helped Native Americans?

☆ How have these laws hurt Native Americans?

Hint: Look in the Readers' Guide to Periodical Literature, under "Indians of North America," for articles about court decisions and laws passed in the last 20 years concerning Native Americans.

Read at least one article about recent laws, then write a one-paragraph summary of the article. Next, write a short skit that dramatizes the issues raised in the decision or law. Your dialogue should include a description of the problem and how it was or is being resolved. With your partners, present your skit to the class.

Hint: Reread the article you have summarized, noting the "main characters" and the issues involved in the making of the law. Use this information in your skit.

Extending Your Studies

MATH

Your task: *To create a class pie graph that shows your class's favorite sports.* A pie graph is an effective way to demonstrate how the parts of a whole relate to one another. For example, once Shirley Hill Witt determined whether or not Native and non–Native Americans in South Dakota received the same sentences for crimes, she could use a pie graph to clearly display her findings.

You can use a similar graph to show your findings on the topic of your class's favorite sports. To make a pie graph, follow the same procedure that Witt did. First, one person should count the number of students in your class. Then, everyone should write his or her favorite sport on a small piece of paper. (Each student may name only *one* sport.) A committee of students should count the students who have named each sport and write the totals on a piece of paper or on the chalkboard.

Next, create a class pie graph to present your findings. The whole graph or "pie" represents all the students (100 percent) in your class. Each "slice" of the pie represents the percentage of students that likes each sport. For example, if your class of 30 people has 15 baseball fans, 10 football fans, and 5 soccer fans, your pie graph would look like this:

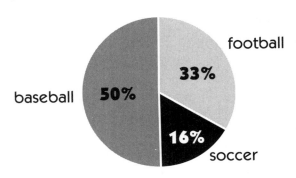

Translate your numbers into percentages and divide your pie accordingly. Finally, display your chart in a class Hall of Fame.

LANGUAGE ARTS **Your task:** *To give a two-minute oral presentation to the class about a community leader whom you respect.* In this unit, you have read about people who work in public service. These people help protect the rights of everyone. Think of another person whose public service you admire. This person could be a government leader, a spokesperson for a cause, or a local activist. Go to the library to find out more about that person. You might begin by answering these questions:

☆ With what issue is this person most concerned?

☆ How did this person become involved in the issue?

☆ What is the exact nature of the work this person does?

Once you have answered these and other questions, prepare a two-minute oral presentation. You might organize the presentation chronologically—according to when significant events occurred in this person's life. In summary, tell why you admire this person. If possible, show a picture of the person to your class.

SOCIAL STUDIES **Your task:** *To write a proposal for a law that would help protect the environment.* Billy Frank's biography shows that private citizens can work to have unfair laws changed and suggest laws that protect the environment. Work with two or three other students to discuss concerns you have about your community's environment. Choose one issue and write a sentence that explains it. Then brainstorm ideas for laws that could help solve the problem. Select the best idea and write a one-paragraph proposal for the law. Then write a letter from your class to your local representative, presenting your ideas. Enclose all your proposals and the reasons your ideas should be enacted.

WRITING WORKSHOP

In Units 2 and 3, you wrote biographical sketches of a friend and a family or community member. The information for these sketches came from memory or interviews. For this sketch, you will use books, magazines, and other sources to write a **researched biography.**

PREWRITING

The first step is to choose your subject. Whom have you read or heard about who interests you? Use the prewriting strategies you learned in Units 1–3 or try one of these suggestions to get started.

Ask questions: Think about what you want to learn about particular fields. For example, imagine that you saw a TV program about water pollution. You found it fascinating, but you know very little about the subject. List questions you have about the field and the people in it.

Another approach would be to start with people. For instance, you might list questions about Native Americans you have read about in newspapers or in this book.

Finally, you might go to the library and look through magazines and books for ideas. List the people who catch your attention. Then narrow your focus to one person you feel is noteworthy and for whom there are enough source materials. Here are some guidelines for your research:

Limit your topic: Do not try to cover the person's entire life. Concentrate on one or two turning points and significant events.

Locate your sources: Most of your research can be done in the library. You will want to explore sources like these:

☆ Card and Computer Catalogs: books listed by title, author, and subject.

☆ The *Readers' Guide to Periodical Literature:* magazine articles on many subjects.

☆ Other Indexes: The *New York Times Index, Art Index,* and *Science and Technology Index,* among others.

☆ Dictionaries and Encyclopedias: specialized references, such as *Current Biography, American Women Writers,* and *Reference Encyclopedia of the American Indian,* among others.

Take notes: As you read, take notes on 3 x 5 note cards. On each card, write the title, author, publisher, date of publication, and page number of the book or magazine you use. Write your notes in your own words. If you want to quote someone, be exact and be sure to use quotation marks.

Organize your notes: First, arrange your notes in categories. Some groups might include Early Life, School Days, or People Who Influenced My Subject. Decide what information you will keep and what you will leave out. Focus on your purpose: What do you want your readers to learn about the person? Check all facts and figures.

Second, organize your ideas in a logical order. Chronological, or time, order can help you tell your story in a way your reader can easily understand.

Finally, decide on an interesting way to start your biography. You could catch your reader's interest by beginning with a quote from your subject, an important event in the person's life, or an intriguing question.

DRAFTING

Now that you have organized your notes, *draft* your biography. Remember that you need not worry about making it perfect. Just get your ideas down on paper. You will check for word usage and spelling errors later. Include a bibliography of all the sources you used.

Include a bibliography: At the end of your biography, list the materials you used in alphabetical order. Use the following form:

Books:

Author	Title	City Published	Publisher	Copyright Date
Smith, Charles.	Alberta Grace.	New York:	Overland Press,	1992.

Magazines:

Author	Article Title	Magazine Title	Date	Page Numbers
Field, Renee.	"Dispensing Hope."	Lives Today.	30 April 1991:	55–57.

REVISING

Put your biography aside for a day or two. Then, with the help of another student who will act as your editor, evaluate and *revise* your work. See the directions for writers and student editors below.

Directions for Writers: Read your work aloud, listening to how it flows. Then ask yourself these questions:

☆ Does my opening hold my reader's attention?

☆ Are the ideas presented in a logical order?

☆ Did I include vivid details?

☆ Have I included quotes from the subject?

☆ Does my writing focus on turning points?

Make notes for your next draft or revise your work before you give it to a student editor. Then ask the student editor to read your work. Listen carefully to his or her suggestions. If they seem helpful, use them to improve your writing when you revise your work.

Directions for Student Editors: Read the work carefully and respectfully, remembering that your purpose is to help the writer do his or her best work. Keep in mind that an editor should always make positive, helpful comments that point to specific parts of the essay. After you have read the work, use the following questions to help you direct your comments:

☆ What do I like most about the biography?

☆ Is the writing clear and logical?

☆ Do the subject's achievements and character come through?

☆ Has the writer used vivid details to describe the subject?

☆ Does the writer reveal why this person is noteworthy?

☆ What would I like to know more about?

PROOFREADING

When you are satisfied that your writing says what you want it to say, check it carefully for errors in spelling, punctuation, capitalization, grammar, and usage. Then make a neat, final copy of your researched biography.

PUBLISHING

After you have revised your writing, you are ready to publish or share it. Create a class book of *Special People, Special Achievements*. Divide the class into small groups to handle various bookmaking tasks.

☆ designing and creating a cover jacket

☆ organizing the book into several chapters

☆ writing the title page, contents page, and an introduction to the book

Then bind the biographies to make a book. After everyone in the class has had a chance to read it, lend the book to the school library for others to read.

GLOSSARY

PRONUNCIATION KEY

Vowel Sound	Symbol	Respelling
a as in *hat*	a	HAT
a as in *day, date, paid*	ay	DAY, DAYT, PAYD
vowels as in *far, on*	ah	FAHR, AHN
vowels as in *dare, air*	ai	DAIR, AIR
vowels as in *saw, call, pour*	aw	SAW, KAWL, PAWR
e as in *pet, debt*	eh	PEHT, DEHT
e as in *seat, chief*; *y* as in *beauty*	ee	SEET, CHEEF, BYOO-tee
vowels as in *learn, fur, sir*	er	LERN, FER, SER
i as in *sit, bitter*; **ee** as in *been*	ih	SIHT, BIHT-uhr, BIHN
i as in *mile*; **y** as in *defy*;	eye	MEYEL, dee-FEYE,
ei as in *height*;	eye	HEYET
o as in *go*	oh	GOH
vowels as in *boil, toy*	oi	BOIL, TOI
vowels as in *foot, could*	ŏŏ	FŎŎT, KŎŎD
vowels as in *boot, rule, suit*	oo	BOOT, ROOL, SOOT
vowels as in *how, out, bough*	ow	HOW, OWT, BOW
vowels as in *up, come*	u	UP, KUM
vowels as in *use, use, few*	yoo	YOOZ, YOOS, FYOO
vowels in unaccented syllables (schwas) *again, upon, sanity*	uh	uh-GEHN, uh-PAHN, SAN-uh-tee

Consonant Sound	Symbol	Respelling
ch as in *choose, reach*	ch	CHOOZ, REECH
g as in *go, dig*	g	GOH, DIHG
j as in *jar*; **dg** as in *fudge*; **g** as in *gem*	j	JAHR, FUJ, JEHM
k as in *king*; **c** as in *come*;	k	KIHNG, KUM,
ch as in *Christmas*	k	KRIHS-muhs
s as in *treasure*; **g** as in *bourgeois*	zh	TREH-zhuhr, boor-ZHWAH
sh as in *ship*	sh	SHIHP
th as in *thin*	th	THIHN
th as in *this*	th	THIHS
z as in *zero*; **s** as in *chasm*	z	ZEE-roh, KAZ-uhm
x as in *fix, axle*	ks	FIHKS, AK-suhl
x as in *exist*	gz	ihg-ZIHST
s as in *this, sir*	s	THIS, SER
wh as in *white*	wh	WHEYET
h as in *who, whole*	h	HOO, HOHL
gh as in *rough, laugh*	f	RUF, LAF
ph as in *telephone*	f	TEHL-uh-fohn

abandonment (uh-BAN-duhn-muhnt) *n.* being completely forsaken or left alone, 47

abstract (ab-STRAKT) *adj.* representing an idea rather than an actual object, 66

abundance (uh-BUN-duhns) *n.* a great amount, 209

access (AK-sehs) *n.* the right to enter or approach, 211

activist (AK-tuh-vihst) *n.* a person who takes positive, direct action to solve a political or social problem, 193

adapted (uh-DAPT-uhd) *v.* adjusted to new conditions, 210

administers (ad-MIHN-ihs-tuhrz) *v.* manages or directs, 7

adobe (uh-DOH-bee) *n.* sun-dried brick made from earth and sand, 27

algebra (AL-juh-bruh) *n.* a type of mathematics in which symbols are used to represent numbers, 154

amateur (AM-uh-chuhr) *adj.* someone who does something for the pleasure of it, not for the money, 73

ambiance (AHM-bee-uhns) *n.* a feeling that goes with a certain person, place, or thing; atmosphere, 36

ambiguous (am-BIGH-yoo-uhs) *adj.* not clear; indefinite, 26

anthropology (an-throh-PAHL-uh-jee) *adj.* pertaining to the study of humans, especially their physical and cultural characteristics, 191

appalled (uh-PAWLD) *v.* filled with shock or horror, 201

artifacts (AHRT-uh-fakts) *n. pl.* objects made by humans; often tools, vessels, and weapons, 30, 192

aspiring (uh-SPEYER-ihng) *v.* to be ambitious or striving toward, 46

assimilate (uh-SIHM-uh-layt) *v.* to become like others, 127

assumed (uh-SOOMD) *v.* to suppose or take for granted, 173

assumption (uh-SUMP-shuhn) *n.* anything taken for granted, 120

astounded (uh-STOWND-ihd) *adj.* very surprised; astonished, 17

atomic energy (uh-TAHM-ihk EHN-uhr-jee) energy that is released from atoms when they are broken apart (fission) or joined (fusion), 145

audition (aw-DIHSH-uhn) *n.* a test performance to see if an actor, musician, or other performer is suited for a job, 93

bribe (BREYEB) *v.* offer money or favors to get someone to do something illegal, 202

candidate (KAN-duh-dayt) *n.* someone who is qualified for the position he or she seeks, 156

careening (kuh-REEN-uhng) *v.* to be lurching or tilting from side to side, 76

celebrated (SEHL-uh-brayt-ihd) *adj.* famous; often talked about, 100

chronic (KRAHN-ihk) *adj.* occurring over a long period of time, 63

clan (KLAN) *n.* a group of people who have a common ancestor and common interests, 210

coexist (koh-ihg-ZIHST) *v.* to live together peacefully, 102

collaborated (kuh-LAB-uh-rayt-ihd) *v.* worked together in some artistic or scientific endeavor, 47

collage (kuh-LAHZH) *n.* an artwork made up of many different materials, 102

colleagues (KAHL-eegz) *n. pl.* fellow workers, 182

commemorates (kuh-MEHM-uh-rayts) *v.* honors; keeps the memory of something alive, 185

commission (kuh-MIHSH-uhn) *n.* a document issued by the President, making a person an officer in the U.S. armed forces, 75

compensate (KAHM-puhn-sayt) *v.* make up for, 8

composure (kuhm-POH-zhuhr) *n.* calmness of mind or manner, 76

consequence (KAHN-sih-kwehns) *n.* importance as a cause or influence, 91

consistency (kuhn-SIHS-tuhn-see) *n.* the texture and weight of something neither solid nor liquid, 130

consolation (kahn-suh-LAY-shuhn) *n.* comfort; something that eases sadness, 182

consulting firm a business that offers advice and recommendations, 138

contemporary (kuhn-TEHM-puh-rair-ee) *adj.* of the present time; modern, 176

controversial (kahn-truh-VER-shuhl) *adj.* causing a great deal of disagreement, 38

credentials (krih-DEHN-shuhlz) *n. pl.* proof of a person's learning or experience, 137

credit (KREHD-iht) *n.* the ability to borrow money, 194

curator (KYOO-rayt-uhr) *n.* a person who decides what will be displayed in a collection or exhibit, especially for a museum or library, 173

derogatory (dih-RAHG-uh-taw-ree) *adj.* tending to lessen or belittle, 28

dilemma (dih-LEHM-uh) *n.* a difficult choice, 18

discipline (DIHS-uh-plihn) *n.* branch of knowledge, 191

disheartening (dihs-HAHRT-uhn-ihng) *adj.* causing to lose courage, 156

diversity (duh-VER-suh-tee) *n.* variety, 67

documentary (dahk-yoo-MEHNT-uh-ree) *adj.* presenting an account of real events, 104

encountered (ehn-KOWN-tuhrd) *v.* met unexpectedly; came upon, 211

ensure (ihn-SHOOR) *v.* to make sure or certain, 211

eradication (ee-rad-ih-KAY-shuhn) *n.* doing away with, destroying, 12

estimate (EHS-tuh-mayt) *v.* to judge the approximate size, number, weight, or cost of something, 191

evoke (ee-VOHK) *v.* to bring to mind; to recreate in an imaginative way, 36

exhibiting (ehg-ZIHB-iht-ihng) *v.* presenting or showing, usually in a museum or gallery, 175

exodus (EHKS-uh-duhs) *n.* the departure of many people, 127

extinct (ehk-STIHNGT) *adj.* no longer alive, 11

Famous Artists Course a course of study offered through the mail that teaches the techniques of well-known artists, 101

fetus (FEET-uhs) *n.* the unborn young of animals and humans, 94

financial aid (feye-NAN-shuhl AYD) money awarded to needy students so they can pursue college educations, 157

flourished (FLER-ihsht) *v.* grew and developed strongly, 127

fossils (FAHS-uhlz) *n. pl.* the preserved remains of something that lived long ago, 30

foster families families who care for the children of others on a temporary basis, 101

fraternity (fruh-TERN-uh-tee) *n.* a group of young men joined by common interests; a Greek-letter college organization, 74

fulfillment (fool-FIHL-muhnt) *n.* realizing one's dreams or ambitions, 47

generate (JEHN-uh-rayt) *v.* to cause to be; to produce, 138

Georgia O'Keeffe (1887-1986) a major U.S. artist who began painting in New Mexico in 1929, 83

grants (GRANTS) *n. pl.* money from the government and other organizations for special programs or projects, 156

immune (ih-MYOON) *adj.* protected against something disagreeable or harmful, 74

infant mortality (mawr-TAL-ih-tee) the death of newborn babies, 103

inhibiting (ihn-HIHB-iht-ihng) *adj.* restrictive; limiting, 18

initiative (ih-NIHSH-uh-tihv) *n.* responsibility for taking the first step; ability to act independently, 200

inspire (ihn-SPEYER) *v.* to have an effect on someone or something, 83

instilled (ihn-STIHLD) *v.* to put in an idea little by little, 64

integrate (IHN-tuh-grayt) *v.* unify; bring together, 27

interact (ihn-tuhr-AKT) *v.* to act on one another, 136

interdependent (ihn-tuhr-dee-PEHN-duhnt) *adj.* connected by mutual need, 136

interview (IHN-tuhr-vyoo) *n.* a formal meeting held to determine a person's qualifications for a position, 155

intricate (IHN-trih-kiht) *adj.* having many different parts, 20

intriguing (ihn-TREEG-ihng) *adj.* fascinating; interesting, 119

judo (JOO-doh) *n.* a Japanese sport, and a means of self-defense that does not use weapons, 183

kiln-fired (KIHL-FEYERD) *adj.* baked at a very high temperature in a kiln oven, 130

landfills *n. pl.* areas set aside for garbage, 136

legacy (LEHG-uh-see) *n.* something handed down from an ancestor, 177

legitimately (luh-JIHT-uh-muht-lee) *adv.* in a real way, 28

lobbied (LAHB-eed) *v.* tried to influence or convince, 221

logo (LOH-goh) *n.* a picture or symbol that is associated with a person or business, 138

mainstream (MAYN-streem) *adj.* dominant or most common, 18

maneuvered (muh-NOO-vuhrd) *v.* guided with skill, 209

martial (MAHR-shuhl) *adj.* showing readiness to fight; warlike, 183

matter (MAT-uhr) *n.* the basic material from which all things are made; matter takes up space and can be seen or sensed in some way, 145

mechanical (muh-KAN-ih-kuhl) *adj.* as if produced by a machine; very carefully made, 84

medicine man a man, usually a Native American, who prevents or treats illness with herbs, songs, dances, and other traditional methods, 82

mediocre (mee-dee-OH-kuhr) *adj.* neither very good nor very bad, 139

memoirs (MEHM-wahrz) *n. pl.* essays that tell about a person's experiences, 21

mesas (MAY-suhz) *n. pl.* flat-topped mountains with steep sides, 128

minutely (meye-NOOT-lee) *adv.* in very small detail, 84

monosyllables (MAHN-oh-sihl-uh-buhlz) *n. pl.* words of one syllable, 10

mortar (MAWR-tuhr) *n.* a mixture of plaster, sand, and water that holds bricks or rocks together, 35

multidisciplinary (muhl-tih-DIHS-uh-pluh-nair-ee) *adj.* pertaining to many different fields of study, 193

mural (MYOOR-uhl) *n.* a large scene or design painted directly on a wall, 84

mythical (MIHTH-ih-kuhl) *adj.* imaginary; not based on facts or scientific study, 45

naive (nah-EEV) *adj.* innocent; unaware, 121

negotiate (nih-GOH-shee-ayt) *v.* to discuss and come to an agreement, 121

negotiator (nih-GOH-shee-ayt-uhr) *n.* a person who discusses issues and tries to bring people into agreement, 204

nomadic (noh-MAD-ihk) *adj.* wandering; moving from place to place, 17

nomads (NOH-mads) *n. pl.* people who do not have a permanent home, but travel from place to place, 145

nonlinear (nahn-LIHN-ee-uhr) *adj.* not understood by reasoning and logic; creative, 44

obsessive (uhb-SEHS-ihv) *adj.* focused on one thing, 104

oral history historical information that is gathered and preserved in spoken form, often passed down from one generation to the next, 174

overturn (oh-vuhr-TURN) *v.* to defeat or reverse, 219

panelists (PAN-uhl-ihsts) *n. pl.* a group of people gathered to judge, discuss, or ask questions, 119

panorama (pan-uh-RAM-uh) *n.* an unlimited view in all directions, 17

pastel (pas-TEHL) *adj.* pale; light in color, 65

perfectionist (per-FEHK-shuhn-ihst) *n.* a person who strives to make things perfect, 129

perseverance (per-suh-VIHR-uhns) *n.* continued, patient effort, 74

persists (puhr-SIHSTS) *v.* refuses to give up; continues a certain practice, 94

pesticides (PEHS-tuh-seyedz) *n. pl.* chemicals used to destroy pests, 221

phenomena (fuh-NAHM-uh-nuh) *n. pl.* events and experiences that can be scientifically explained, 146

phonetic (foh-NEHT-ihk) *adj.* representing speech sounds, 148

pigments (PIHG-muhnts) *n. pl.* materials used to color; paints, 82

potent (POHT-uhnt) *adj.* effective or powerful in action, 73

potential (poh-TEHN-shuhl) *n.* hidden talent, 155

powwow (POW-wow) *n.* a ceremony or conference of Native Americans to help cure disease or celebrate success, often with feasting and dancing, 76

practical (PRAK-tih-kuhl) *adj.* workable; of everyday use, 137

precision (prih-SIHZH-uhn) *n.* accuracy; exactness, 193

prestigious (prehs-TIHJ-uhs) *adj.* having the power to impress or influence, 17

prominent (PRAHM-uh-nuhnt) *adj.* widely and favorably known, 174

propagated (PRAHP-uh-gayt-ihd) *v.* reproduced or spread, 20

punctuated (PUNGK-choo-ayt-ihd) *v.* interrupted or occasionally disturbed by something, 48

qualifications (kwawl-ih-fih-KAY-shuhnz) *n. pl.* knowledge, skills, or experience that enables someone to do a job, 202

rally (RAL-ee) *v.* to bring back into action, 184

rebelliousness (rih-BEHL-yuhs-nuhs) *n.* active resistance to authority; defiance, 183

rehabilitation (ree-huh-bihl-uh-TAY-shuhn) *adj.* bringing someone or something back to health, 92

relent (rih-LEHNT) *v.* become more agreeable, less stubborn, 201

resources (REE-sohrs-uhs) *n. pl.* natural sources of wealth, 218

restored (rih-STOHRD) *v.* brought back to its former condition, 82

revered (rih-VIHRD) *v.* regarded with deep respect, 219

scripts (SKRIHPTS) *n. pl.* the written text of plays, movies, or TV shows, 94

segregated (SEHG-ruh-gayt-ihd) *adj.* set apart or separated from others, 26

shaman (SHAH-muhn) *n. pl.* spiritual leaders and healers, 154

siblings (SIHB-lihngz) *n. pl.* brothers and sisters, 63

significance (sihg-NIHF-uh-kuhns) *n.* importance, 219

Sioux (SOO) *n.* refers to the Oglala Lakota nation of Native Americans, 76

skeptical (SKEHP-tih-kuhl) *adj.* not easily convinced; doubtful, 93

slipshod (SLIHP-shahd) *adj.* careless, 193

spawning (SPAWN-ihng) *adj.* places where eggs are laid, 219

stereotypes (STEHR-ee-uh-teyeps) *n. pl.* rigid ideas about a person or a group that allow for no individual differences, 10

stumped (STUMPT) *adj.* puzzled; confused, 119

supplement (SUHP-luh-muhnt) *v.* to add to, 173

tolerant (TAHL-uhr-uhnt) *adj.* showing respect for others' beliefs and practices, 26

tranquility (tran-KWIHL-uht-ee) *n.* the state of being free from troubles or worries, 37

treaty (TREE-tee) *n.* an agreement or contract, 219

troupe (TROOP) *n.* a company or group of actors, singers, or dancers, 10

unanticipated (un-an-TIHS-uh-payt-ihd) *adj.* unexpected; unforeseen, 8

undaunted (un-DAWNT-ihd) *adj.* not discouraged, 101

undertakings (un-duhr-TAY-kihngz) *n. pl.* the actions of a person who attempts to do a project, 38

utilities (yoo-TIHL-uh-teez) *n. pl.* companies that supply homes with electricity, natural gas, water, and other services, 146

venture (VEHN-chuhr) *n.* a risky or dangerous undertaking, 11

veterans (VEHT-uhr-uhnz) *n. pl.* people who have served in the armed forces, 201

vitality (veye-TAL-uh-tee) *n.* energy; liveliness, 8

vulnerable (VUL-nuhr-uh-buhl) *adj.* open to damage, 20

BIBLIOGRAPHY

Begay, Fred

Gridley, Marion. *Indians of Today.* Chicago: ICFP Inc., 1971.
"The Long Walk of Fred Young." *NOVA* (#602) Journal Graphics, 267 Broadway, New York, NY 10007.

Campbell, Ben Nighthorse

Mazanec, Jana. "The American Dream: Campbell Wins Primary." *USA Today,* Aug. 13, 1992, p. 2A.
Moss, Desda. "40 Years Later Congressman Gets His Diploma." *USA Today,* May 1, 1991, p. 2A.

Frank, Billy

Egan, Timothy. "Indians and Salmon: Making Nature Whole." *New York Times,* Nov. 26, 1992, p. C1.
Rede, George. "Nisqually Indian Leader Will Receive Schweitzer Award." *Oregonian,* Oct. 12, 1992, p. B8.

Geiogamah, Hanay

Geiogamah, Hanay. *New Native American Drama: Three Plays.* Norman: University of Oklahoma Press, 1980.
Lincoln, Kenneth. "A *MELUS* Interview: Hanay Geiogamah." *MELUS,* Fall 1989, pp. 69-81.

Grant, Rodney

Spillman, Susan. "The Wind Lifts Grant's Career, Costner's 'Dances' Completes Star's Turn." *USA Today,* Nov. 30, 1990, p. 4D.
Grant, Rodney. "Stars in Stripes." *Redbook,* July 1991, p. 65.

Harjo, Joy

Harjo, Joy. *Secrets from the Center of the World.* Tucson: University of Arizona Press, 1989.

Jaskoski, Helen. "A *MELUS* Interview: Joy Harjo." *MELUS,* Spring 1989, pp. 5-13.

Hill, Rick

Cembalest, Robin. "Pride and Prejudice." *ARTnews,* Feb. 1992, pp. 86-91.

Dorris, Michael. "His Mission? An Indian Museum Like No Other." *New York Times,* Sept. 13, 1992, sec. 2, p. 53.

Mills, Billy

Bloom, Mark. "The Greatest Upset." *Runner's World,* Aug. 1991, p. 22.

Distel, Dave. "It Took 20 Years, But Mills Finally Gets To Celebrate." *Los Angeles Times,* May 14, 1986, sec. 3, p. 1.

Momaday, N. Scott

Katz, Jane B., ed. *This Song Remembers: Self Portraits of Native Americans in the Arts.* Boston: Houghton Mifflin Co., 1980.

Momaday, N. Scott. *The Way to Rainy Mountain.* Albuquerque: University of New Mexico Press, 1976.

Qöyawayma, Al

Gianelli, Frank. "Tops in Four Fields." *Graduating Engineer,* Oct. 1984, pp. 24-28.

Rose, Wendy

Commire, Anne, ed. "Rose, Wendy." *Something About the Author* series. v. 12. Detroit: Gale Research, 1977.

Rose, Wendy. *The Halfbreed Chronicles and Other Poems.* Albuquerque: West End Press, 1985.

Ross, Mary

Brandt, Linda. "Mary Ross: A Pioneer." *The Minority Engineer,* Spring 1984, pp. 87-88.

Segundo, Tom

Gridley, Marion. *Indians of Today.* Chicago: ICFP Press, 1971.

Stocker, Joseph. "Tom Segundo: Chief of the Papagos." *Arizona Highways,* April 1951, pp. 18-25.

Silko, Leslie Marmon

Katz, Jane B., ed. *This Song Remembers: Self Portraits of Native Americans in the Arts.* Boston: Houghton Mifflin Co., 1980, pp. 186-194.

Silko, Leslie. *Almanac of the Dead.* New York: Viking Penguin, 1992.

Smith, Jaune Quick-to-See

Herzog, Melanie. "Building Bridges Across Cultures." *School Arts,* Oct. 1992, pp. 33-34.

Porum, Jennifer P. "Jaune Quick-To-See Smith." *Artforum International,* Jan. 1993, p. 87.

Steele, Lois

Cortright, Barbara. "Recipient of Tradition." *Southwest Profile,* Aug. 1985. pp. 21-24.

Steele, Lois. *Medicine Woman.* Grand Forks: University of North Dakota, 1985. (Write to: INMED, 501 North Columbia Rd., Grand Forks, ND 58201.)

Velarde, Pablita

"Pablita Velarde." *American Indian Arts Magazine,* Spring 1978.

WalkingStick, Kay

Malarcher, Patricia. "The Meanings of 'Duality in Art.'" *New York Times,* Dec. 22, 1985, sec. 11, p. 16.

WalkingStick, Kay. "Native American Art in the Postmodern Era." *Art Journal,* Fall 1992, pp. 15-17.

Weber, Laura

Simonelli, Rich. "An Interview with Laura Weber." *Winds of Change,* Autumn 1992, pp. 98-103.

Witt, Shirley Hill

Commire, Anne, ed. "Witt, Shirley Hill." *Something About the Author* series. v. 17. Detroit: Gale Research, 1979, pp. 247-8.

Green, Rayna, ed. *That's What She Said: Contemporary Poetry & Fiction by Native American Women.* Bloomington: Indiana University Press, 1984.

Wittstock, Laura

Wittstock, Laura. *Sugarbush: Ojibwe Maple Sugar Making.* Minneapolis: Lerner Publications, 1993.

CAREER RESOURCES

Unit 1: Literature and Drama

These magazines present students' and adult writers' work, and articles that discuss the craft of writing.

The Horn Book (includes book reviews for young people)

Stone Soup (a literary magazine for young people)

Story (a literary magazine for advanced readers)

Writer's Digest (features articles about ways to improve writing and interviews with writers)

Unit 2: Fine Arts and Performance

The following magazines explore the concerns and happenings of the art world.

American Art (profiles American artists)

American Artist (discusses artistic techniques and materials)

Architecture (features prominent architects and their work)

Asian Art (concentrates on Asian artists)

You might also look for this book about Native American art in your library.

Highwater, Jamake. *Many Smokes, Many Moons: A Chronology of American Indian History Through Indian Art.* Philadelphia: J.B. Lippincott Company, 1978.

Unit 3: The Sciences and Engineering

To learn more about science and health, watch for *NOVA* specials on public television. These programs discuss scientific breakthroughs and interview scientists. You might also enjoy the following magazines:

American Health (presents news in medicine and health)
Byte (for and about computer programmers)
Discover (news of science)
The Futurist (theories of the future)
Popular Science (the mechanics of scientific instruments)

You can also contact this agency for information about careers in the sciences and engineering.

AISES (American Indian Science & Engineering Society), 1630 30th St., Suite 301, Boulder, CO 80301; (303) 492-8658

Unit 4: Education and Public Service

These agencies can give you more information regarding specific problems, careers, or issues raised by this unit's biographies.

National Congress of American Indians, 900 Pennsylvania Ave., Washington, DC 20003; (202) 546-9404

Native American Public Broadcasting Consortium, P.O. Box 83111, Lincoln, NE 68501; (402) 472-3522

Native American Rights Fund, 1506 Broadway, Boulder, CO 80302; (303) 447-8760

For up-to-date news on government, politics, and economics around the world, look for the magazines *Newsweek, Time,* and *U.S. News and World Report.*

INDEX